FAMILIES AGAINST THE CITY

RICHARD SENNETT

Families against the City

MIDDLE CLASS HOMES OF

INDUSTRIAL CHICAGO

1872–1890

VINTAGE BOOKS

A Division of Random House

New York

VINTAGE BOOKS EDITION, October 1974
Copyright © 1970 by the President and Fellows of Harvard
College

Library of Congress Cataloging in Publication Data

Sennett, Richard, 1943–
Families against the city.

Reprint of the ed. published by Harvard University
Press, Cambridge.
Bibliography: p.
1. Family—Chicago. 2. Middle classes—Illinois—Chi-
cago. 3. Chicago—Social conditions. I. Title.
[HQ557.C5S45 1974]   301.44′1   74–4293
ISBN 0–394–71089–4

*this book is dedicated in appreciation
to my teachers
Erik Erikson and Oscar Handlin*

ACKNOWLEDGMENTS

This study has been supported by grants from The Joint Center for Urban Studies of Harvard and M.I.T., The Woodrow Wilson Foundation, and The Graduate School of Arts and Sciences of Harvard University. I should like specially to thank Professor Daniel P. Moynihan of the Joint Center for Urban Studies and Dean Thomas K. Sisson of the Harvard Graduate School for their assistance in speeding this study on its way.

Social research has become largely a cooperative venture, and my debts to others are great. I should particularly like to thank Thomas Stuart, my research assistant, for his diligent help during all phases of the data collecting, and for his good-humored skepticism about the supposedly scientific aspects of our work. I should also like to thank the programmer for this study, Edward F. Kelly, for donating so much of his time to the project, and for generating a protocol of analysis for the data much advanced over previously existing methods.

Many friends have read the earlier drafts of this study, or discussed the project with me at length. I should like to thank Stephan Thernstrom and Charles Tilly for their comments on the entire manuscript, and David Riesman for valuable suggestions about the social setting of the data.

ACKNOWLEDGMENTS

Ilse Ounjian, Pat D'Addio, Sona Caro, and Carol Cofrancesco spent many hours translating my illegible scrawling into a finished manuscript.

My greatest debts are to my teachers Erik Erikson and Oscar Handlin. They have been generous with their time and interest, and their thinking has had an impact on my own far beyond the boundaries of this particular study. I should especially like to acknowledge my debt to Oscar Handlin for his unflagging support in guiding this study from beginning to end, and for giving me a great deal of advice of the best kind, advice that enlarged, rather than limited, my own freedom of thought.

Finally, I should like to thank my wife for her good humor and support during the course of this research.

CONTENTS

CONTENTS

Part Three
Social Mobility
and Intense Family Life

MAPS

FAMILIES AGAINST THE CITY

INTRODUCTION

One of my great delights as a boy, when I would make an occasional pilgrimage to Chicago from our house in Minnesota, was to take a tour of the city with my uncle in his car. He knew all of Chicago and seemingly all there was to know about it, so that we would make lengthy excursions, comparing the grandeur of the thin line of the Gold Coast with the decay and squalor of the enormous areas that lay just behind it, or driving slowly through Maxwell Street, our progress blocked by street vendors and sidewalk merchants who made of this place an old-world peasants' market.

One area I remember particularly was "Union Row" on Ashland Avenue, part of the near West Side. In what looked to be mansions were the homes of the Chicago trades locals; the large bay windows were filled with announcements of strike votes and elections, and beyond, in the elegant interiors of these homes, one expected the walnut paneling and beamed ceilings to enclose rooms of Tiffany glass and delicate settees, but found instead unshielded fluorescent lights over rows of metal desks. There is an entire colony of homes such as these in the area, of which Ashland Avenue's Union Row forms the far western edge, a cluster of houses whose solidity and respectability manages to make itself still felt, even though the inhabitants are now hoboes rooming close together, or very old people whom society has abandoned to poverty.

I wish I could claim always to have harbored a secret desire to find out how such elegance came to so sorry an end, but my attention quite accidentally returned to this old neighborhood in looking for a scene, a locale, in which I could study a more wide-ranging problem.

Today the majority of Americans live in that amorphous region between poverty and wealth called the middle class, yet little is known of how the conditions of middle class life have developed over the course of time. And although the majority of middle class people live in or near cities, the relation between the city and the growth of the middle class is virtually unknown.

The supposed obsession of middle class people in America with rising "to the top" in their work is one of the easiest clichés of social commentary. But this is a society where not everyone can be at the top; most people can at best be partial successes, by bettering their circumstances little by little over the course of their lives. The intriguing subtlety in this doctrine of success is what happens when it fails to be all-absorbing, so that men seek other centers of interest and achievement for themselves. In particular, what kind of investment do such men, between the extremes of poverty and wealth, make in their family lives? Surely, the family is the arena outside of work in which all men can have a chance to express themselves, and it seems reasonable that the conduct of family life must bear some relation to the conduct of work. But these interrelations are obscure; they are important questions about which very little is known.

The matter is further complicated because "family" and

"work experience" are not grand powers that hold sway over men's lives in a vacuum, but are shaped by the kind of human settlement in which men find themselves situated, be it farm, village, or city. Since the majority of Americans have come in the last century to live in large cities, some complex triad of city life, family, and work must give shape to the lives of middle class people in this country. But for all our vaunted arts of self-scrutiny, few men would venture to say how this triad is constructed.

The intent of the present study is to make a small contribution to this unexplored area, through examining the conditions of family life for one group of middle class people at the point in America, during the decades after the Civil War, when the massive cities took form. Since so little is known of middle class people at this time, a broad analysis of national or international trends would be impossible; rather, study of a particular middle class urban community seemed to me at the outset of my research a better way into the problem. After some preliminary exploration, I realized that the decayed Chicago community of which I have such vivid memories from my childhood was during the decades of industrial growth after the Civil War one of the largest middle class neighborhoods in the city, with a population principally composed of native-born bankers and lawyers, clerks, bookkeepers, store owners, and office workers. Within this neighborhood on the near West Side most of the grades between rich and poor were to be found, but few of the rich and few of the industrial poor made their homes here.

A person's family and job are such elemental conditions of life that it might seem that the traditional modes of the historian's craft would inevitably be adapted to analyzing them. This is not, unfortunately, the case. As is true in many efforts in urban studies now, the boundaries of the present work are defined not so much by the lines of one discipline as by the character of the urban subject matter itself. If, as occurs in this study, a father's work experience is explored in its impact on his relations with his wife and children, the result is not a combination of sociology and psychology in historical perspective; these are separate kinds of knowledge by convention only. The experience of people has a unity of its own, and must be studied as a whole.

In addition, the nexus between family and work in the lives of these middle class people would be difficult to explore using the ordinary technique of historical research, the analysis of descriptive documents. Since the people in this Chicago area were unexceptional, few chronicles of their lives were written, and fewer of what documents once existed have survived into the present day. The documents themselves were usually unsuitable for a task like this: they were seldom in a standardized form that permits disciplined comparison between large numbers of individuals; thus, it is difficult to determine what a group of people might have experienced as a whole.

A different kind of historical record is needed to explore the relations of family and work in this city community. Thanks to the technology of the computer it is now possible to take advantage of unusual historical records to explore such a problem previously immune to research.

The present study is divided into three parts. The first is a history of family life in the area called Union Park, from its orgins to just before the Chicago World's Fair of 1893. The sources of this portrait are documents and commentaries, contemporary newspapers, and related secondary sources. Here are introduced a set of problems about family and work that the traditional sources do not answer; Part One is more of a prelude, a raising of the issues, than a comprehensive local history. The second and third parts of the study explore in greater depth the families who lived in Union Park. In these sections, the techniques of demography — the statistical description of a community — are used to explore the meaning of family and work in Union Park over the course of two decades.

In the second part of the study, personal census records on all Union Park families, comprising 12,000 people, are analyzed for the year 1880. This second part forms a cross-sectional portrait, with a large number of social traits studied as intensively as the census records and the computer through which they were processed permitted. In the third part of the study, all fathers and sons at work in 1880, about a thousand people, were tracked down in city directories from 1872 to 1890. The purpose of this eighteen-year trace was to follow through the issues that emerged from the intensive study of family and work during one year. In the long-term trace, the occupational and geographical mobility of these thousand people was mapped out. The resulting occupational and residential histories were related to the characteristics of family life which these Union Park residents possessed at a midpoint, in 1880. In this way I hoped to show how the conditions of family life influenced, and were influenced by, work life over nearly a score of years.

The issues ultimately dealt with in this study are emotionally charged ones. The study tries to show how an intense and warm family life under certain conditions destroyed bonds between father and son, destroyed as well the strength the members of the family possessed to deal with the urban world around them. As such, the study is a critique of a certain kind of middle class life that took form during this seminal period of city growth. Yet I have not sought in this book to "make paste of the middle class".

as the French student phrase goes; that effort leads nowhere. For better or worse, the majority of people today are middle class and will remain so. It is more important to find out how middle class people can realistically achieve some measure of dignity in their lives than to engage, as is so common in the United States, in criticism of the bourgeoisie simply to show how vulgar or sterile it is. The charges may be true, but tell nothing of what might be changed.

The statistician reading this report is bound to be somewhat disappointed. Because so little is known about middle class families, I have deliberately sought in the final chapters to speculate as broadly as possible about the data from Union Park. Anxious precision in a new field such as this can only serve to inhibit true intellectual exploration; there are so few sure guides on which to rely. In addition, although I have used the computer to hold a great deal of information I could never hope to hold in my head, much of my "data" is too precarious or uncertain at its origin to be subjected to scientific analysis by the machine. This study contains, for example, no factor analysis, but only frequency distributions and simple cross-tabulations between variables. A computer is just as much a boon to the student of society as to the scientist, but a different kind of boon. The diversity and complexity of social phenomena are lost through applying exactly those techniques which uncover the diversity and complexity of natural phenomena — or so it has seemed to me, as a result of numerous wrong starts made in this study in search of statistical rigor and logical clarity.

Part One

PROLOGUE: THE DEVELOPMENT

OF UNION PARK'S HOME LIFE

1

THE FULLNESS OF LIFE:

UPPER CLASS FAMILIES IN UNION PARK

BEFORE THE GREAT FIRE

When Chicago was little more than a trading outpost, the families of Union Park, clustered on Chicago's western edge, formed a small and quite comfortable community known for a certain aristocratic calm in the midst of the hurry of provincial town life.

In later years, when the little town had become a giant city filled with enormous offices and stores at its center and grimy, prisonlike factories at its fringes, the community of Union Park would lose its tranquil isolation, and the "decent" families would flee to other havens within the city. The decline and fall of city neighborhoods, however, is seldom the work of a day or a year. A quarter of a century intervened between the era when only the best families lived in Union Park and the time from the 1890's on when only the worst families lived there; in this quarter century there was a middle class hegemony in Union Park, composed of respectable families of "nondescript" character, years in which Union Park and its environs on the near West Side became "the social Brooklyn of Chicago." [1] It is the hidden family life of these nondescript people that constitutes the subject of the present study.

The first years of affluence in Union Park cannot be separated from such an enquiry, for the impact of upper class life on Union Park did not end when the upper class families themselves faded from the scene. The lingering association of these families with the Union Park "image" made the area attractive to the middle class when, through a peculiar combination of circumstances, the community became economically accessible to them as a place to live. More important, the family lives of the early upper class were a yardstick against which to measure the character of those families of lesser means who subsequently crowded into the wide boulevards and secluded side streets of this residential neighborhood.

Attempts to weigh the differences between the age of affluence in Union Park and its subsequent decay were first made by those early residents given to writing memoirs. From H. C. Chatfield-Taylor, a leader of Chicago society two generations back who grew up in the Union Park neighborhood, came a characteristic recollection: "One must be truly an Old Chicagoan to recall the time when the shady streets which lie west of the river vied in social standing with any in the city. Here factories now belch their smoke upon the mansard roofs of dilapidated tenements that once were the mansions of wealthy citizens whose scions blush for their origin." [2]

What is interesting in accounts like Chatfield-Taylor's, or that of Carter Harrison II, a son of a Chicago mayor who himself served as mayor, is that the area seems to have sheltered from its inception a band of fashionable families that had extensive face-to-face relations with each other as a community.[3] To use a more sociological term, a diverse network of "primary-group" bonds and affiliations marked

10

this area; small social clubs, philanthropic committees, established lines of party-giving and other entertaining, sprang up. The result was that the family unit was only one arena, although an extremely important one, in which the original inhabitants of the community had face-to-face social contact with each other. In the middle class era that followed, this diversity of primary-group networks in Union Park disappeared, and the family group became the center of social activity. In the process of this shift in communal focus, the family group changed its character radically. Studying the nature of the upper class homes provides comparative tools to measure the family life of the middle class people who subsequently came to dominate Union Park.

The existence of a diversity of primary-group associations in Union Park from its beginnings was due to the economic geography of the city in the 1830's and 1840's.

How Union Park Came into Being

An 1883 guidebook to Chicago, as charming as it is inaccurate, provided this account of how the West Side came into its own: "The early Chicago had the lake shore for a breathing place, the boundless prairies for a ramble, and the little public square, with its rustic town pump, for a mall, and with these they were satisfied, until one day in 1853 Mrs. Carpenter put it into the head of her husband and Reuben Taylor to have a park on the West Side." [4] It is true that for many years Chicago was little more than a village at the edge of the lake, but one doubts the power of even so formidable a lady as Mrs. Carpenter to command her husband to buy several square miles of real estate and build a large park, simply on the whim of a day. In fact, Carpenter's advent on the West Side came

11

twenty years before, in the 1830's, and was a monumental failure; but a failure that in its turn helped another group of men develop the area for residential use.[5]

One of the earliest residents of the near West Side, Charles Cleaver, built a house four blocks west of the Chicago River, which, he later wrote, "at that time (1838) seemed a long way out of town." The house stood for many years alone on the prairie, almost like an outpost.[6] But undeveloped land in the area was owned by individuals in extensive parcels. In particular, Philo Carpenter owned a large tract of land near the future Union Park worth over a million dollars a few years later, and Samuel Walker owned a smaller amount, about 150 acres, in the same area.[7]

The Panic of 1837 marked the beginning of the real-estate development of this community, for it set events in motion that provided the economic base for residential building in the area by entrepreneurs. The Panic put an intolerable burden on the finances of Philo Carpenter, so that he was reduced to selling his million-dollar parcel of West Side real estate for $8500 to settle a debt of that amount.[8] This area, known as "Carpenter's addition to Chicago," creditors took in one transaction, including as part of the deal his magnificent house, at Randolph and Carpenter streets, a landmark in the city. A large parcel of land thus fell into the hands of men eager to develop the property all at once rather than, as Carpenter had done, allow it to lie fallow as the grounds of a suburban mansion.[9]

The geography of Chicago determined the desire of developers to erect in one stroke a whole community in this part of the city. Most large cities are located on or near rivers; in the case of Chicago, the Chicago River's two branches converge at what was then the center of town.

In the nineteenth century, the river was used as an open sewage and refuse canal; that meant it smelled. To someone with a sensitive nose and ample means, it was an obvious move to get as far away from the river as possible, on open high land like that of the West Side.

There was an equally important, though less obvious, reason why the geography of Chicago should have favored development of the West Side in the years before the Great Fire. Homer Hoyt, a leading analyst of the early development of Chicago, has singled out communication with the central business district as being of equal importance with the river's location in determining where wealthy people lived at this time.[10] The near West Side possessed a particularly favored position in the forties, fifties, and early sixties in its communication with the central business district and the city's resources located there.

The major business area of Chicago up to the end of the Civil War ran east to west through the middle of the city along Lake Street (see Map 1). Transport links — streets, and the hansom cabs, horse trolleys, and coaches that traveled them — tended to orient themselves along this east-west axis. As business and population grew, streets stretched out further to the west, rather than massing in the same area to the north and the south. The condition of the other regions of the new city in part accounted for this linear development. The near North Side above this business district was still largely unfilled and swampy; the South Side awaited the growth of commuter transport on the Illinois Central Railroad to establish a secure link with the city's center. So it was natural that western extension of the city, which was really a lengthening of the commercial flow of the central business district, not a changing of its axis, should proceed rapidly, and that those looking for a home easily accessible to the downtown, but away from the noisome river and the close city quarters, should begin to build on the West Side.[11]

Thus Carpenter's tract was very quickly developed by a small group of investors, much as is a modern suburban tract. But these men wanted to live in the area for the very reasons that made it desirable property to other wealthy people. Carter Harrison tells us that they therefore tried to sell as many as possible of the lots and finished homes to their friends, most of whom came from Kentucky and Virginia.[12] Thus were a homogeneous band of people, with pre-established ties in many cases, brought together; the development of Union Park made possible in this way the easy establishment of diverse kinds of face-to-face associations and bonds.

How Families Lived

THE IMPORTANCE OF THE PARKS. The parks of nineteenth century American cities were places of active public resort, places where fashionable men and women of the day went to see and to be seen. The design of these parks strikes many modern viewers as a little ludicrous; miniature Chinese pagodas are set in the middle of duck ponds, Gothic moats and meandering pathways abound; every element seems to be drawn from the world of childhood fantasy rather than from the adult urban world outside the park. Yet it is exactly the fantastic element that, in the hands of a great designer like F. L. Olmsted, could justify a park's reason for being; the fantasy of these spaces made them places of escape and rest from the crudity, the stench, and the gridiron dullness of the new American cities.[13]

The near West Side's parks were very much a part of the fantastic refuge tradition inaugurated in James Bigelow's Mt. Auburn Cemetery in Cambridge, Massachusetts, and consummated in Olmsted and Vaux's design for Central Park. In the two parks in the area — Union Park, comprising nearly fifteen acres, and Jefferson Park, comprising six acres — were to be found the ponds for swans, the little castles, the miniature Chinese temples, of the American Gothic park.[14] Union Park was completed in early 1854; Jefferson Park was finished in 1850.[15]

A park of fantasy like Union Park provided a focus of recreation and a social meeting ground outside the boundaries of the home. For children, the large land mass and Gothic planning provided all manner of diversions; it was a controlled area of play with special things to do or see, rather than simple relief from the streets and sidewalks.[16] For adults, the park served a double function. It provided a place for neighbors to meet, to see each other and to be seen; and it established a meeting ground between the residents of this area and other affluent people in the city.

Because of the transportation advantages of the western portion of Chicago, its wide, well-paved boulevards, its easy access to and from the central part of the city, the parks of the West Side became a natural meeting ground for polite society when it went out "to take the air" and keep tabs on itself. Carter Harrison II remembered, for example, the concerts given in Union Park on Saturday afternoons and their relation to the fashionable life of the city: "In Union Park of a summer Saturday afternoon, concerts were frequently given between the hours of five and seven by Voss' band . . . While the band played, the fashion of the neighborhood paraded in fine array, some strolling, some driving slowly in wide, open landaus, the populace looking on in rapt admiration. Union Park was the Bois de Boulogne of the West Side." [17] The comparison to the Parisian park was not so fanciful; in both places, a sparsely settled quarter of the city became the fashionable region in which to show oneself off. With the opening of the West Side Driving Park, the drive through the parks of the West Side became a very fashionable form of recreation. In this way, Union Park avoided the claustrophobia of a modern suburb; there was a natural focus for people in the community to meet and socialize with people of the city.

Though the near West Side of Chicago never acquired a special name of its own in the nineteenth century, the character of these parks, creating so much social life for both children and adults, suggests that the little band of homes lying around Union Park might reasonably be named for the park itself, and so it shall henceforth be called.

LIFE IN AN UPPER CLASS HOME. The two good extant memoirs of Union Park in its heyday are distinguished not by the class but by the different interests of their authors. Carter Harrison II was a man bent on the pleasures of good food, good talk, and travel. He described the patterns of social contact in this community from the viewpoint of one who thoroughly enjoyed them. A. C. Chatfield-Taylor seemed a more quiet and private soul, though his communal activities were as varied as Harrison's. He was not given to relating whom he knew and the good times he had with his friends, but, rather, set on evoking the tone and feeling of homes and families, evoking the private circle of their lives. In this way, the two memoirs complement each other as pieces of local history; the personal divergences of the authors marked out two different sections of a common social terrain.

Chatfield-Taylor's account stressed the gulf between the social leaders of Chicago on the West Side before the Civil

War, and the industrial moguls and their society that grew up along the lake's edge a generation later. This divide might be characterized as that between a restrained, elegant upper class in the prewar period and an upper class of magnificence in the later decades. Tangible signs of this divide were to be seen in the architecture of the West Side homes built before the Civil War, where there was an absence of imposing display, an absence of what came to be regarded as "grand." Many of these homes, now defaced beyond recognition or razed by the bulldozer in an attempt at urban "renewal" through the destruction of fine architecture, were marble fronted town houses resembling the town houses still extant in New York on the south side of Gramercy Park. To the modern eye the homes indeed look elegant, but to Chatfield-Taylor's generation they were much more "proper," due to their simplicity, than the houses of wealthy men in Chicago, built in the 1880's and 1890's. In the early marble-fronted town houses, nothing except for mansard roofs was borrowed from abroad to give a foreign tone; there were no stone turrets, Renaissance fronts, or English half-timbering.

The architecture of Union Park reflected a most salient characteristic of the family life of the community: its primness and uprightness. This upright quality formed one of the grounds on which the community thought of itself as upper class.[18] Such a linking of superior virtue to superior class status in American cities is a familiar image of the times; it was given strong expression, for example, in the portrait Edith Wharton made of the Van Der Leydens of New York in *The Age of Innocence*. In Union Park, the conduct of the family group was the way this union between virtue and status was expressed. Absent in these homes before the Civil War was the industrial baron's acquisition of a sumptuous house sumptuously furnished, a sign of his personal power in the work world of the market and factory.[19] For the earlier generation of urban elite, one's ability to limit display, to avoid pomp, was the mark of "tone" and breeding. A "rigid simplicity" dominated the house itself and life of the family within. The roles of husband, wife, and children were all defined so that material and emotional restraint would prevail in an atmosphere where the forms of family association were fixed and unchanging.

A simple upper class household in Chatfield-Taylor's day included a cook, a "second girl" to do housework, and a "hired man" to drive the family carriage and do the harder menial labor. Dinner was served at noon, and at this midday meal the father presided, coming home from the office to do so. These meals were for the family alone; on only one day during the year did Chatfield-Taylor remember his house open before evening to visitors for dining — the New Year's Day celebration that was the high mark of the social season.[20]

For stricter families, dancing and cards as well as horse racing and the theater were forbidden. These families attended Wednesday night prayer meetings, and refused to go to boxes at the elegant new Crosby's Opera House. Only one festivity, New Year's Day, was convivial for all: "Throughout the remainder of the year we staid West-Siders, being firmly convinced of our social and moral excellence, led commendable lives." [21]

The leader of this staid propriety was the father. He was the ruler, the lawgiver, and the children treated him not with easy familiarity, but with trembling respect. The instrument of the father's power in the family was the church; his leadership in the church was a sign of his own virtue, and his family were expected to obey him since it was he who voiced and embodied the laws of religion.[22]

This authoritarian, father-centered rule was becoming unusual in American homes at the time, as will later appear in this study; and within Union Park's confines, while the father-centered pious home was the norm, certain exceptions to the rule could be found. A group of "fast young men," Chatfield-Taylor recalled, refused to follow the lead of their fathers, and instead of attending Sunday church, normally the highpoint of the week, they scandalized their elders by speeding trotting horses past the church doors.[23] These fast young men were to be seen at the new opera house; they attended the gaming resorts of the city, and frequented the houses of prostitution that catered to a wealthy clientele. Chatfield-Taylor said of such young urban aristocrats that "these Sabbath-breakers were without our social pale," which was in one sense true, for they were undoubtedly considered beneath the virtuous elect. But these "fast young men" could not be so simply dismissed as *declassé;* they were the vanguard of a new generation of Chicago leaders for whom the pleasures of the city were to be explored, not disdained.[24] Significantly, the Union Park West Side community did not offer such men the facilities they required. The opera was not located here, nor were the concerts of the new orchestra of Theodore Thomas; the "society" of the West Side, resting on social groups at the scale of the church or small club, was of a wholly different, more personal character, than the large-group, urbane amusements of the next generation.

For Chatfield-Taylor's parents and their circle, the pristine, restrained houses on West Washington Street and around the parks were an ideal setting for the restrictive life they led. One could drive in the park, but the atmosphere was of a fantastic, childlike place, everything screened by trees. The Chicagoans of Dreiser's *Sister Carrie* would resort to such refuges, but they met also in the gilded Palmer House, in crowded clubs and theaters.

Because the rules of family life were in these wealthy Union Park residences formal and rather austere, it did not follow that the families were isolated, inward-turning societies; their piety did not lead to seclusion. On the contrary, families like Chatfield-Taylor's enjoyed a lively and extensive social life, a social life of a peculiar character and charm.

The memoirs of Carter Harrison II, whose family was close to Chatfield-Taylor's, recalled this social life with great verve. To Harrison, social life during the early years of Union Park was "hopelessly crude." Apart from the daytime use of the parks, social amusements consisted mainly in the form of dancing and eating, and the setting of these pleasures was usually within private homes.[25]

Social occasions were a mixture of generations. In the very earliest days of the community, the "merrymakers" were young married couples whose children, as they grew up, were gradually incorporated into the parties of the elders, and at a certain point supplanted them in social activity like dancing, which was not quite appropriate for corpulent, middle-aged burghers.[26]

Let us try to re-create the atmosphere of a supper dance in one of the homes of the West Side during the halcyon years, at the house of the H. H. Honorés, a prominent family in early Chicago. Their mansion "served as a landmark of the West Side; its breezy air of hospitality, its jutting bay windows, its spacious pillared front porch, its cupola, and its cheery, smiling grounds are still remembered by many old-time Chicagoans." [27] The Honorés belonged to a social organization called the "Grasshoppers," a social club that sponsored dances in the various homes of the community. In such a home-centered atmosphere, dancing would go on from after dinner until about eleven P.M. for the young, while the older people sat by and watched or talked; then the band of the evening would play a supper march, as all the guests moved in a kind of stately procession to the dining room for a huge feast.[28]

The height of the social season for members of the Grasshoppers was New Year's Day. Practically every family kept open house, and it was again the pleasures of the home table and bar that were the center of activity. Eventually the round of New Year's calls was abandoned because of occasional drunkenness. In the next generation of Chicago society, both drinking and dancing moved into public places of assembly, where unruliness could not demean the dignity of the home, an unruliness that was becoming more than occasional as dances grew larger, with the growing population. Receptions and balls in the home did not, of course, cease, but the impersonal grand balls, the great feasts and gentlemen's parties, could be more convivial and unrestrained in a rented hall where no one's domestic sanctity could be ruffled during the course of an evening. Before the Civil War, such amenities did not exist on the West Side, nor was the desire for great crowds of guests, all admiring the grandeur of a hostess who could accommodate them, the fashion.

Harrison indicated that the community was quite stable during its early years; a common circle of friends, stretching between and across generations, constituted the neighborhood of Union Park. He dates the exit of the H. H. Honorés from the area in 1866 as the beginning of the removal of fashionable families from the West Side; evidently before that there were no prominent shifts in the community that signaled a trend of outward movement.[29]

A Peculiar Noblesse Oblige

The wealthy burghers of Union Park lived a staid, proper, socially active life within their homes. These homes were immune from the ills of the city: the miseries of the poor did not disturb the view from the bay windows of the mansions or town houses, nor were the signs of commerce present in any noxious form. Originally, both the Chicago stockyards and a boisterous tavern, the Bull's Head, were located close to Union Park. By the early 1850's, the area was purified of both institutions and their transient population; in their place grew up retail and service businesses much more restricted in scope, much more of an amenity than an incursion on the neighborhood.[30]

Some pockets of poverty and factory industry were taking form about a mile south and west of Union Park in the 1850's and 1860's. In an embryonic stage, these areas began to surround the prosperity of the residential area with factories, a poor industrial proletariat living in crowded conditions, and areas of crime and vice.[31] In the era before the Great Fire there was only a suggestion of what would come; the rich did not rub shoulders with the poor, the ride from the community into the center of the town was still pleasant, not yet a trial.[32]

The wealthy citizens of the near West Side did not in fact ignore these first symptoms of blight. They tried to deal with them in a manner characteristic of the ideas by which they shaped their own lives. In the early period of affluence for the Union Park community, the emerging pockets of poverty in the surrounding areas were not taken as a threat, because poverty was not seen as a permanent, ineradicable condition of human life. Unlike the great social workers of a later generation, the first residents of the area were bent on helping poor people enjoy an urban life that originated outside the culture of poverty, not one that took place within its terms.[33]

Their attitudes led them to try to change the lives of very poor or unfortunate people by direct exposure to members of the "better" classes. A number of voluntary organizations were set up to create social change through personal reform. This was the rationale for the location of the Washingtonian Home for Female Inebriates on the site of the old Bull's Head Tavern, adjacent to the estate of H. H. Honoré, near the home of the Carter Harrisons and the Chatfield-Taylors, looking into the backyard of the Ogdens. If anything would help these unfortunate women, surely living among such scions of Chicago would, surely the frequent visits of Mrs. Honoré and her daughters and the other women of the community would provide an example and an ideal of virtue to which the drunken women might aspire. Similarly, when Dr. George Shipman opened a foundling home for deserted children at 54 S. Green Street, just before the Great Fire, these orphans were expected to benefit morally from contact with young boys like Carter Harrison II or little Hobart C. Chatfield-Taylor as they played together in Union Park, near the duck pond shaded by trees, or explored together the wonders of the animal zoo.[34]

These attempts at charitable uplift showed a certain openness to the poor and their problems. Destitution was a personal misfortune, not an element of the social structure, and these scions of Chicago were willing to let the unfortunates taste the bracing upright qualities that knitted together their own family lives. The history of the community's attitudes toward urban poverty moved from this open help to a defensive walling in of the middle classes, who later occupied the near West Side, against those who had gotten what they "deserved" in the industrial and commercial marketplace.

The early attitude toward the poor reflected as well the importance the wealthy Union Park families put on direct, primary-group contacts in the moral relations between people. It is thus of a piece with the attitude such families as Chatfield-Taylor's had toward proper social relations within their own circle and with other wealthy families in the city. In this network of primary groups, the place of the family was that of defining virtue and virtuous activity through self-restrictive behavior. The rules of the family were the criteria through which the young people of the community would learn to deal with each other, for the family taught self-discipline, respect for authority, and the value of personal relations. The family unit did not come to absorb all social life of a face-to-face sort within its bonds; it rather dictated how primary-group relations of "our circle" were to be conducted.

All this changed in Union Park in the late 1860's and 1870's. A family life took form that can be understood as the mirror opposite of the style of these first years, and among a new class of people. The causes of this change were to be found not in the character of either the first families or the early community institutions of Union Park, but in larger urban forces which played on this community apart from its will or control.

2

A CHANGE IN OBJECTIVE CONDITIONS:

WHY UNION PARK BECAME

A DIFFERENT COMMUNITY

Three Forces of Change

POTTER PALMER HAS AN UNUSUAL IDEA. In the spring of 1868, Mr. Potter Palmer, wealthy Chicago drygoods merchant and Civil War financier, had good reason to feel pleased with himself. A long trip to Europe during the previous year had restored his flagging health; his bank balance was fattened with the proceeds from short-term loans to the government during the recent conflict; and he had no business responsibilities, having sold his flourishing store to Field and Leiter before going to Europe. Now, with so much in his favor, he could retire to a life of leisure and sport, and in middle age enjoy the fruits of a successful young manhood; this, indeed, everyone in Chicago expected him to do.[1]

But he did not. Perhaps the boredom of leisure began to distress him, perhaps the itch for making money was too firmly implanted for him to stop once he was rich. In the spring of 1868, Potter Palmer re-entered the world of business, but not business as he had done it in the old days.

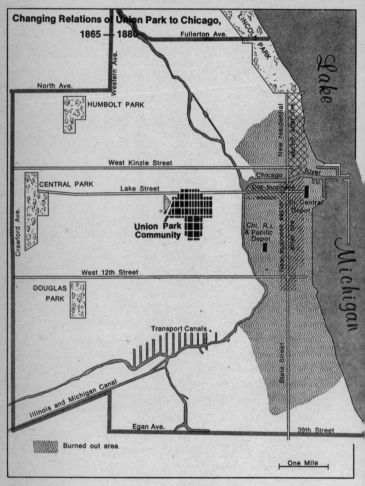

Changing Relations of Union Park to Chicago, 1865 — 1880

Fullerton Ave.

LINCOLN PARK

Lake

Western Ave.

North Ave.

HUMBOLT PARK

West Kinzie Street

CENTRAL PARK

Lake Street

Crawford Ave.

Union Park Community

Chicago

Old business section

New residential area after fire

River

Central Depot

Chi. R.J. & Pacific Depot

New business section after fire

Michigan

West 12th Street

DOUGLAS PARK

Transport Canals

Illinois and Michigan Canal

State Street

Egan Ave.

39th Street

Burned out area.

One Mile

MAP 1

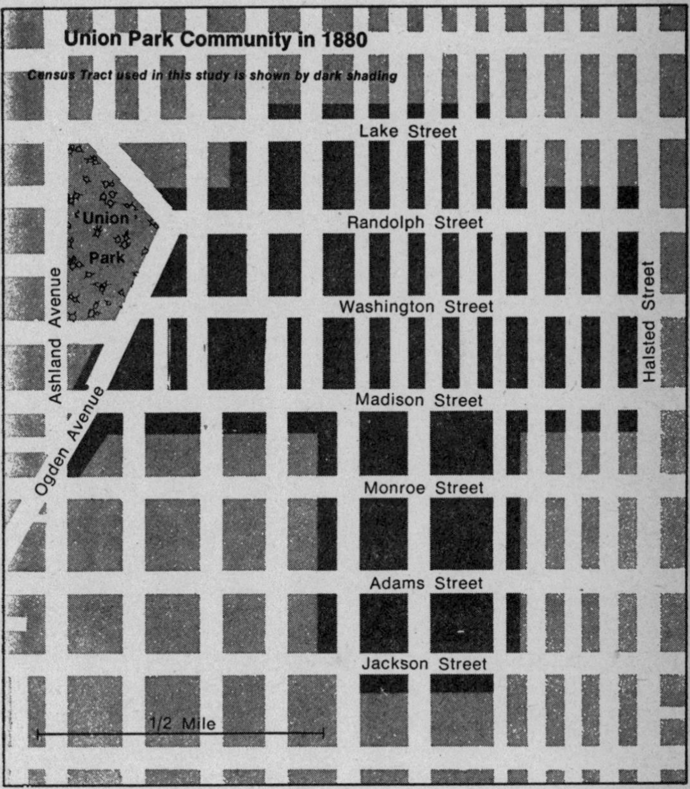

Union Park Community in 1880

Census Tract used in this study is shown by dark shading

Union Park

Lake Street

Randolph Street

Washington Street

Madison Street

Monroe Street

Adams Street

Jackson Street

Ashland Avenue

Ogden Avenue

Halsted Street

1/2 Mile

MAP 2

Potter Palmer had had what people called an "unusual idea," and it led him into city real estate, not back to the old ways of storekeeping.

Palmer's scheme was to have an enormous effect on the life of Union Park. The idea was very simple. Palmer wanted to change the central business area of Chicago from its east-west axis along Lake Street by turning it ninety degrees so that the line of development was north-south along State Street.

At first conservative businessmen in Chicago could not believe that State Street, which was then a narrow alley, paved with stone chips and poorly lighted, could ever vie with the well-developed commercial area along Lake Street. Here is how a friend of Palmer's remembered the street at the time Palmer proposed to develop it: "State Street, then narrow, ill paved, below the city grade, with irregular jobs and pavements which were lined by squalid one story frame buildings, occupied by saloons, black-smith shops, second-hand dealers, boarding houses for labourers, etc., presented a most forbidding aspect." [2] Yet it was to this street that Palmer turned, buying up about a mile of it north of Twenty-second Street at a price of less than a dollar and a half per square foot.[3]

Why get involved in such a venture? The biographers of Palmer list his reasons for changing the axis of commercial development from east-west to north-south as though they should have been self-evident propositions at the time.[4] In retrospect, Palmer's plan was not the only rational path for future development. There was plenty of room for the central city to grow as it had in the past. But, as in the case of railroad capital, the rationale for real estate development and rational reasons for growth were often in this period distinct; there was a passion to build, buy, and borrow among the capitalists of the time that far outstripped the needs and credit resources of American communities.[5] In the years immediately after the Civil War, Chicago investors were a band of enthusiastic innocents, eager for a big, quick killing, more inclined to follow club-room rumor and inside tips, to emulate those like Potter Palmer who had already made it big, than to consult in quiet their own common sense about what they could afford to risk.

So when Potter Palmer made his unusual idea known to the public, after an initial round of disbelief it became common wisdom that the wave of the future for investors was indeed in land lying north-south, that the east-west development of the city up to the time of Mr. Palmer's announcement had been "unnatural," a "mistake," and a "dead end" for growth. The pace of change induced by the new wisdom was furious.

A residential change in the city soon favored this new commercial axis, and it was again the work of Palmer. In July of 1870, Potter Palmer married Miss Bertha Honoré, daughter of the H. H. Honorés. The new Mrs. Potter Palmer was intelligent, witty, very much a snob; she was born to be a grande dame who would dictate and define fashion. But she did not rule Chicago society under the terms the old families of Union Park approved. Mrs. Palmer displayed a love of costly jewelry, of imposing staircases, of rooms crowded with treasures from the old world. She was bent on establishing her social superiority through displaying the magnificence her husband's wealth could command, not, as was true for Chatfield-Taylor's parents, through leading a more upright life than any of the neighbors.[6] Such a woman fit very well the tastes for grandeur Potter Palmer himself displayed.

The couple built a house on the near North Side that became famous throughout Chicago for its opulence and the magnificence of its social gatherings. Their mansion had a great impact on opening up this lakeside region for fashionable residential development. Palmer filled land near the lake that was swampy, and soon the area was primed for the crowding of the very rich along the north-south axis of the city, on the edge of the lake, that persists in present-day Chicago.[7] Palmer's location of his home in this new place may not have been dictated simply by business reasons. Yet it is inescapable that, were the axis of business development to be turned north and south, the roads out of the new central district had to have somewhere "good" to go.[8]

This commercial and residential change had a strong impact on the relation of Union Park to the city center. To the end of the Civil War Union Park had direct, rapid transport to all sectors of the central business district; now with the axis turning at right angles to the old flow of traffic, unpleasant changes were occurring.

The first shift was occasioned by the loss of retail businesses on the older streets, on Lake, Washington, and Madison. This business section was suddenly inundated by wholesale trade which "rushed into the vacuum created by the withdrawal of the retail and financial interest from Lake Street." [9] The effect of this was to prevent a fall in the price of land, indeed to keep it stable; socially, however, the change in the kind of business conducted meant that the commuters going down the old avenues of traffic had a different experience in reaching the central city.[10]

Streetcars on Madison and on Lake still were connected to the central business district, for they stopped at the end of the line at State Street, but one had to pass through an area of warehouses, shipping depots, and lorry stations; even more, the warehouses came to be flanked by establishments that the retail character of the streets formerly had prohibited. In open streetcar or carriages one had now to pass through block after block of men drinking in bars, prostitutes roaming the streets for early pickups, occasional brawls, and then through the "ghost" areas of the old commercial streets, once crowded with life, now much more empty, with buildings boarded and barred at the first story, with lorries and carts disrupting the flow of traffic into downtown.[11] Palmer's "unusual idea" meant that in place of the older sense of geographic distance that separated the Union Park area from the central city, there now grew up a sense of social isolation. In the earlier period, one covered socially neutral, nondescript territory in reaching the center of the city and many central-city dwellers came out to enjoy Union Park's lawns and greens. The result of re-orienting the business axis was that the old commercial area became empty of life but the areas contiguous to it acquired a definite social character, usually associated with the "warehouse-flophouse" fringe. There arose, as a result of Palmer's scheme, a kind of social wall between the West Siders and the city's center; it was penetrable, but to do so was not pleasant.[12] Thus did the attractiveness of the area begin to decline in the minds of the "best people."

The force of Palmer's venture on Union Park, however, like so much else in Chicago's early industrial history, cannot be understood apart from its relation to the Great Fire of 1871, which literally razed the city to the ground.

THE FIRE. Since the superlatives in modern usage are used every day for everyday things, it is hard to evoke the feeling of a catastrophe like the Great Fire of 1871 in Chicago. Almost the whole city burned, so that at the fire's height, many square miles were simultaneously ablaze. The only thing people could do to cope with the holocaust was to flee it, and this hundreds of thousands did across the Chicago River to the western part of the city.

Because the river acted as a natural boundary, the homes of the West Side were spared the flames, along with a few homes far to the south. This fact played a decisive role in changing the character of communities like Union Park. In the immediate wake of the fire the West Side served as a refugee area for the enormous numbers of displaced persons of the city; Chatfield-Taylor, for one, remembered quite vividly what this movement of the homeless to his quiet, subdued neighborhood was like: "All day long, too, the homeless trooped through our West Side streets, begging at our doors for food and shelter — some grimly bearing their lot, others in tears, or frenzied with excitement. Over the few bridges that were still unburned they came, driving wagons filled with household goods, or trudging hand-in-hand with crying children, their backs bent to the weight of treasured objects, a baby's crib, maybe, or a family portrait." [13]

The West Side soon became flooded with temporary businesses and families living in emergency quarters, so that its population in the year after the fire was 214,000 people, nearly two thirds the population of the city.[14] All levels of the social stratum crowded into Union Park of necessity; and many who built temporary homes here stayed when the rest of the city was rebuilt. In this way the population increased all at once, just as at Union Park's founding. Most important, the new residents were dominantly of a lower class than the first. That people of modest economic status could afford to stay was the result of both the pattern of rebuilding the city and a second holocaust, the Depression of 1873.

In the weeks after the fire, many expected the West Side to become the central business area of the city, with Halstead and Madison comparable to pre-fire State Street. On the part of Madison Street and its offshoots that lay between the river and Halstead, modest homes were quickly converted into store fronts as their owners rushed to capitalize on the temporarily booming thoroughfare of West Madison Street.[15]

Within a year, however, it became clear that the idea of renewal among Chicago's leaders was not to make experiments in the form of the city but to re-establish business as usual by rebuilding central city and residence areas along patterns developing before the fire.[16] Now, indeed, Palmer's projects for State Street could be easily pursued since all was leveled to the ground; new land along the north-south axis of State Street near the lake could be developed in a coherent manner.[17] This left the commercial enterprises on the West Side in a precarious position; either they would remain as a prosperous second center of retail trade, even though they were outside the city, or they would decline, so that the re-emerging central city would leave an area of ramshackle businesses.

The Depression of 1873–1877 was the event that decided this issue, for it ruined many of these new small businesses, which had not the power to compete against the big merchants downtown, and at the same time lowered residential land values and rents in Union Park. Before the fire, warehouses and a warehouse fringe existed only on the east side of the river; now, in the wake of the fire and the Depression, there grew on the west side of the river, much closer to Union Park itself, another shabby commercial region, decayed and deserted in the restoring of the old central city.

THE DEPRESSION OF 1873–1877 AND ITS AFTERMATH. In 1873 Chicago underwent a financial and commercial contraction that lasted four years. This depression in business was nationwide, and at the national level its origins seemed connected with overextension in railroad investment.[18] In Chicago, the depression in rails alone did not account for business decline; there was, in addition, a failure in the realty market that was to stifle older courses of real estate development, and bring to a halt the growth of such established urban areas as the near West Side.

The course of the decline was as follows. In the spring and summer of 1873, land prices were still booming in the areas surrounding the West Side and South Side parks, but becoming stationary in the older, built-up portion of the city, from Halstead in toward the center of town. During the summer, investment capital began drying up, particularly as skilled-worker wages fell — for after the Fire these men tried to save small sums of money from each paycheck to rebuild their homes, and their small savings in aggregate were a large part of Chicago's capital market.[19] On September 18, the announcement of the failure of Jay Cooke precipitated a stock market crash and a series of bank closings. Land values in the city did not, however, fold immediately, but steadily declined over the next four years. As a result of this slow process of decline, land values in the near west neighborhoods of the city now dropped, as in Union Park, about 50 percent in value.[20]

The effect of the Depression on the near West Side did not stop here, for in the process of gradual renewal of business that began in 1878 certain older areas in the city were avoided by investors, as though it were the fault of the land that the depression had started.[21] In this regard Union Park was the hardest hit:[22] in the course of the depression, it had been marked out by real estate entrepreneurs as an area that would not bode well as a site for future real estate of the "best" kind.

The result of the Depression of 1873–1877 was that the effects of previous events on the relations between Union

Park and the rest of the city were now being reflected in the economic land base within the area itself. The community now began to show economically the results of changes that at first seemed external to it, matters that before seemed unrelated to what parties the Honorés, the Walkers, or the Harrisons would give, or to what band was playing in Union Park on the weekend. For, it must be remembered, the near West Side was still growing and prospering in the five years between the Civil War's end and the Great Fire. The Fire and the Depression must have been to the old families a sobering proposition, as they saw developers cease building "acceptable" homes, near their little parks and on their grand boulevards, and turn to places that were more pleasantly situated in relation to the commercial center of town and more protected from the raucous under-life of Chicago, immediately to the east of Union Park. In place of such acceptable development, a host of temporary or modest dwellings were erected all at once, and the Depression seemed to confirm the fact that this was now about all the community was "worth" for future growth. Thus were the new, middle class people in Union Park ensconced and the old elite encouraged to leave.

The unfolding of these developments in Union Park in the 1870's graphically illustrated an urban process the leaders of the community did not understand: the interdependence, the symbiosis, of distinct regions within an urban whole. Many community leaders were bewildered by events because they imagined themselves able to cope with the social life of "our people" at the local, face-to-face level. But, as the forces shaping the community lay not within its boundaries, the sundry efforts to save it that were centered at the local level were doomed to fail.

The New Middle Class Community

These changes had two immediate effects on the internal structure of Union Park. First, their cumulative impact was to change the dominant class level in the community from upper to middle class. Second, the concentration of population radically increased. This was due to the aftereffects of the Great Fire, and then, as the middle and lower middle classes stayed to settle, due to the fact that the housing stock they could afford did not permit spacious grounds or back yards. It was housing of lower cost than the old, and of higher density.

A tourist walking through the residential streets off Union and Jefferson Parks in 1880 would have encountered a strange sight. Wedged in the back streets off the grand boulevards, or between the mansions on them, were modest houses totally unlike the elegance visible from an earlier era. The streets were in fact crowded with these small apartment houses or single-family homes in between mansions, or in alleys behind the marble-front houses. To be sure, some mansions with spacious lawns were there undiminished also, but it was as though one style of life had suddenly become superimposed on another, the modest life of neat, clean, respectable "little people" crowded among the grand life of some of the city's leading burghers. Because in this era no zoning codes were designed to restrict heterogeneous residential development, the older residents had no protection when the value of their land fell in the Depression of 1873–1877.[23]

To the east, all the way to the Haymarket, such little homes and apartments abounded. At the eastern boundary, few great mansions would be in evidence, but there were many small shops, some studios and art galleries, a few theaters on Halstead Street itself; here the respectable residential area stopped suddenly, for the Haymarket, noisy, unclean, and putrid smelling, a major produce trading center for Chicago, lay beyond, and beyond it were warehouses and a "flophouse fringe."

The Census of 1880 provides some insight on the demographic continuity and differentiation within the dense, middle class community that took form by the end of the 1870's.

Union Park, as I have defined it, was a T-shaped area of some forty square blocks (see Map 2). On its east-west axis, the area extended from the park known as Union Park on the west to Halstead Street on the east; this was a distance of fourteen blocks. North to south, the vertical axis of the T extended seven long blocks. The whole of the area was residential, with no factories and few stores.

In 1880, the population of this T-shaped area was 12,000 people. It is impossible to compare this exactly to the earlier era, because the historical records have been destroyed; based on fragmentary evidence, I estimate the population grew from 600 or 800 in 1860 to 12,000 by 1880, with this segment of the near West Side temporarily sheltering about 40,000 in the year after the Great Fire.[24] In the eastern and western sections of this T, the population was equivalent and more dense than in the central area running north to south. The densities in the east arose for different reasons than those shaping the west. The eastern sector grew during the refugee period after the Great Fire, whereas the western sector grew up earlier, during the upper-class, initial phase of development. But by 1880 modest homes and apartment houses were predominant in both of these populous sectors, as well as in the less developed zone between.

Families of the Halstead Street area and of the area bordering Union Park had a diverging socio-economic charac-

Table 1. The occupations of people living around Union Park and near Halstead Street, 1880

Occupation	Union Park		Halstead Street	
	Number of workers	Percentage of those working	Number of workers	Percentage of those working
High-level white collar (executives, professionals, proprietors)	228	25	140	14
Low-level white collar (clerical, secretarial)	358	40	344	34
Blue collar	152	17	415	41
Household servants	166	18	112	11
Total	904	100 (approx.)	1011	100

ter. Table 1, based on my analysis of the Census of 1880,* shows this difference in terms of occupations of their residents. Between these two sectors there seemed a gulf: two thirds more high-level white collar workers lived around Union Park; more than twice as many blue collar workers lived in the Halstead Street sector. But when these figures are related to the history of the near West Side, and the conditions surrounding it in 1880, the differences seem less significant. Before the Civil War, the families around Union Park were solidly upper class, and much fewer; in 1880, this section was densely packed, and the dominant occupational group was the lower-level white collar worker. On the other hand, the Halstead Street zone was quite different from the decay, the "warehouse-flophouse fringe" located on the other side of the Haymarket; in the Halstead area, the white collar classes were more prevalent than the class of manual laborers. Almost all the servants in both sections

* All tables and graphs in this book are based on my analysis of the 1880 Census or name lists in the Chicago City Directory.

lived in the households of the upper middle class. These historic conditions bound the eastern and western sections together as differing subgroups of one, albeit rough, communal whole; they were hardly the same, but they had come to share a similar occupational dominance — that of those who did not labor with their hands, but were below the occupational elite.

The lower-density area between these east and west sectors was midway as well in its occupational structure. This statistical phenomenon meant that within the whole census area there was no sudden break between the affluence of neighborhood areas, nothing at all comparable to the sudden contrast one experiences now walking a block from the wealth of Central Park West into the slums of the New York Puerto Ricans. The gradient here was smooth, and social contrasts between sections were not suddenly apparent.

A tour through all of the Union Park district would have moved, then, from an area of opulence, fading in the growing presence of petite bourgeoisie, to an area of more mixed class character, but still dominated by the same petite bourgeoisie; across the Haymarket area, two or three blocks yet more to the east, one would have suddenly been in the midst of warehouses and storage vaults. There appears to have been, in general, a fairly even distribution of people of different ages throughout the community in 1880; that is, young people did not predominate in one area, middle-aged in another. In the eastern Halstead Street area, however, there were many more young people who were the heads of a household or who lived alone than in other parts of the community. This meant that there was a greater concentration of young families or of lone young people in the community that grew up along Halstead Street after the Great Fire than in the older, more established parts of Union Park to the west. In the older section around Union Park itself, there was an equal number of young people, but they had not broken away from their parental homes.

The existence in Halstead Street of an art gallery, shops, and a theater, coupled to this age characteristic of the population, suggests that life in the Halstead Street area may have been a little freer than among the staid homes around the park. The young people on the eastern edge of Union Park could live under less restraint because they had broken a bond that those to the west had yet to break; as shall be seen, this special quality of the young people partially explains the socio-economic status of the area.

In its first era, Union Park was composed almost entirely of native-born Americans. In the 1870's, foreign-born people came in small numbers to dwell in the community, but under striking circumstances: native and foreign born lived in conditions of complete residential integration.

Three fourths of all the people in Union Park in 1880 were native-born and one fourth were foreign-born; this three-to-one ratio was found in every sector of the census area. For instance, when the census area was divided into twelve zones of equal land mass, a constant division of native and foreigner occurred in each zone. A closer look within selected city blocks revealed that foreigners did not tend to cluster apart from natives at a more microscopic level. No ghetto pockets were to be found here.

This ethnic integration occurred in part because of the image of the foreigner held at the time, a more complex image than that held by the native middle classes at the end of the century. On the one hand, the foreigner may have been an anarchist, or dark stranger, or lazy alcoholic, but there was still current at this time the sense that America was a shelter to the sturdy people from Europe who wanted or were able to escape the shackles of a backward form of life.[25] Given such an image of the foreigner in America as the hardiest or pluckiest of his lot from his native country, some openness could be possible.

But a more tangible, specific factor was also at work. The point of origin for the majority of the foreign-born in Union Park was northern Europe and about half of these were from countries where English was the common language. The breakdown of nationality groups for the foreign-born in 1880 was as follows.

Percentage of total population	Nationality
6.8	British: England, Scotland, Wales
5.9	German: German states and Austria
4.7	Canadian
4.4	Irish
2.2	Scandinavian
0.7	Latin: Italy, France, Spain
0.2	Slavic: Russia, Poland, Bohemia
0.1	Asian
0.1	Other

In other words, these urban foreigners were "foreign" in a different, less marked way than those who came in the great migrations from southern and eastern Europe a decade later. There were some mutual bonds between migrant and native. Only the Irish among these groups were saddled with a stereotype as a lower order of human being than the native.[26]

The native-born adult elements of Union Park were drawn from the general American centers of population before the Civil War; there was no unusual regional concentration. Most came from the Middle Atlantic states and the

Ohio-Kentucky belt.[27] The American majority of the Union Park people were in this sense "just average" people.

The effect on Union Park of changes in Chicago's structure during the years 1865–1880 has so far been posed in terms of increasing density and a new class structure. The Census of 1880 shows some internal differences and similarities in Union Park under these new social conditions. Statistics do not, however, show the greatest change in the community, a change in the basic social quality of its life.

The hidden effect of Palmer's plans, the Great Fire, and the 1873 Depression was the loss of the old network of multiple primary-group associations. In the new community that emerged in the decade of the 1870's, the family became the sole medium of face-to-face, everyday life. The older voluntary associations for philanthropy withered, however, and new ones did not grow up; church life lost its character as a small band of congregants, and became instead an impersonal rite attended by thousands; the older patterns of hospitality and entertaining were not continued among the new people, nor were extensive "neighborly" contacts forged along new lines. Even the use of public resources like the parks were feared as a potential danger. Few public meeting grounds, like bars or clubs, survived in these years in Union Park.

The reasons why these multiple avenues of face-to-face contact disappeared cannot be explained simply on the grounds of the great numbers and density of people living in the neighborhood, nor simply on the grounds that the new class character of Union Park did not permit entertainments and voluntary organizations of the scale natural to the older residents. The narrowing of primary-group associations occurring as this community became middle class was also the result of changes in the family itself, for during the middle class era of Union Park, the family evolved so that its members did not *want* to establish diverse primary-group experiences for themselves. It is this complex relation between middle class family life and community structure to which we now turn.

3

LITTLE ISLANDS OF PROPRIETY:

MIDDLE CLASS FAMILY LIFE IN UNION PARK

The people who came to live in Union Park in the 1870's did not repeat the style of family life of the community's older households. The newcomers, typed at the time as "respectable but of modest means," or "middle class," could not of course afford the domestic amenities of coachmen or second maids which the older families enjoyed. But apart from these economic differences, there were sharp changes in the relations between people within families, and in the relations between groups of families in Union Park. Why the middle class families were so different, what powers gave shape to their lives, are the puzzles this book seeks to understand.

Neither rebels nor leaders, the middle classes have been, as is so often remarked, the forgotten people of the American city. Because their lives have been the routine norm, rather than the arresting exception, traditional sources of information on them — newspapers, published memoirs, official documents — are wholly inadequate; the only middle class lives men can usually explore are their own. To use a phrase from Marx, they are condemned to the "rim of society" that is the present.

But enough can be dug out of archives and from old books to establish some signs of the family life among these particular middle class people living in a burgeoning industrial city. These signs are what require explanation; like the markings an archaeologist studies from a vanished civilization, these family documents indicated the presence of a certain kind of life, but did not explain it.

The New Family Scene

About six blocks south of Union Park itself, near Ashland Avenue, was the childhood home of Laura Kendall Thomas, who left a short, unpublished memoir of her childhood in the 1870's, now in the collection of the Chicago Historical Society. In one way, Mrs. Thomas' childhood neighborhood was much like that of Carter Harrison II's, twenty years before. Some suburban hallmarks, such as homes with chicken coops, or even with cows grazing in backyards; an uneven, in places sparse, residential development — in some blocks these remained as they were a score of years before.[1]

But whereas the Carter Harrisons lived one house to a block or in town houses with fields as their backyards, Mrs. Thomas lived in a rowhouse development, with no large yards. Her home was part of a high-density housing scheme, built in expectation that this kind of home would fill the unused lots all along the street. Unlike the Harrisons or the Honorés, the Kendalls were renters. Though their $25 a month for two full floors and a basement was a substantial sum at the time, it was well within middle-income range.[2]

Mrs. Thomas' parents had a different kind of boundary to their neighborhood than did the Harrisons. From the doorstep of Mrs. Thomas' childhood home, facing west, was an enormous row of post-fire squatters' huts, stretching up a few blocks toward the park and down toward Twelfth Street; there was undeveloped space, then, but not unused. The squatters on these open lots marked a social boundary that good families like Mrs. Thomas' would not permit their children to trespass. When Carter Harrison stood in the cupola of his house, as a boy, only fields and uncut prairie to the south and the west could be seen; no people "of a different sort" arrested his attention. In 1880 an alien world thus lay at the child's doorstep.

Laura's childhood in some ways was like that of children throughout the American Midwest at the time. She attended school, where she was taught by an elderly and somewhat austere spinster; in class she scribbled painfully at a high desk, in the school yard she played the games of tag and maypole all children played, then and now. But in some ways, her life in Union Park was special. Her parents led her to school and met her at the school yard to take her home; she was forbidden the use of the park, and asked to play near home where her mother could keep a constant watch on her. The uninhibited wandering and exploring that Carter Harrison remembered as a child were not part of her memories; she was much more closely tied to home.[3] This cannot be explained simply as a difference in the amount of freedom accorded little boys and girls at the time; nor by the presence of "undesirables" in the neighborhood. A change in the quality and focus of family life in homes like Laura's was involved as well.

The family life of such Union Park middle class homes was subject primarily to scorn, when, rarely, it received comment from observers or chroniclers of the Chicago scene. The reason for this lay first in the striking relations to be seen in Union Park between husbands and wives, so different from those experienced by a previous generation.

According to the account of a certain F. B. Wilkie, who surveyed Union Park life in 1879, the lives of the relatively prosperous married men and women in this community were cursed with an imbalance of power and authority, in comparison to what existed during the community's upper class years. He described the women as the strong-willed and aggressive ones; the husbands were characterized as "sweet" and "docile," of "retiring disposition." Chatfield-Taylor described the earlier generation of women as following "meekly" in their husbands' paths. In the new community, the wives rather than the husbands were the authority figures.[4]

One striking trait of these "docile husbands" was their withdrawal from a social life outside the home. Their passivity was partially composed, as Wilkie saw it, of their tendency to use the family as the social focus of their lives after work and on weekends, to sit of an evening in the parlor reading the newspaper or to tinker about the garden fixing things. Contacts with their peers outside the house, in voluntary associations, club meetings, and the like, did not seem to be as appealing. The milder, gentler amusements around the family hearth were preferred.

Such tensions as Wilkie observed between retiring husbands and strong-willed wives arose from how the wives felt about themselves as part of the middle class. Behind the wives' vigor was a sense of shame about being just "respectable" and living in a middle class community. The result of this shame was twofold. The wives were constantly pushing the husbands to succeed. The women were led also into pretentiousness. This latter Wilkie chided with a heavy hand: "Every woman on Westside once lived on The Avenue [Michigan or Prairie] in a place known as Southside [the elite part of Chicago]. Whenever she goes to town, she goes to visit a frend on The Avenue. Whenever she has been down town, she has been to call on a friend who lives on The Avenue. A good many ladies who live in Westside carry the idea, in the [street] cars, that they live in Southside on The Avenue, and are only in Westside for a visit." [5]

The more serious tension grew out of the wife's pushing of her husband to improve his job, in order to better the family's position. It may be that the aggressive dominance of these Union Park women was a product of their shame about the family's class status; being ashamed of oneself and one's family finds a natural outlet in aggression, "taking it out" on someone close at hand like one's husband. Yet the reason why the husbands in these homes were so gentle and family-centered is not therefore explained.

The women of Union Park, in this account, were pushing their "docile" husbands to better the family's position, to be mobile upward, through successes in work. Yet passive and gentle men would seem ill suited to achieve such gains. Evidently the issue of occupational mobility brought to a head a deep, psychological tension in the relations between husbands and wives. Some of this tension can be seen in a portrait Theodore Dreiser made of a family lower in the social spectrum of Union Park.

Historians have often been struck by Dreiser's capacity to evoke in a few paragraphs scenes that less gifted imaginations, working in both fictional and nonfictional media, struggled through whole volumes to depict. Dreiser's portrait, in *Sister Carrie*, of a respectable poor family in Union Park is one of these indelible scenes. It occurs early in the novel when a young girl, Carrie Meeber, newly arrived in Chicago from the hinterland, goes to live temporarily with her sister and brother-in-law in Union Park. This married couple, the Hansons, were at the top of the working class. Dreiser placed them in a section of Union

Park where people in more remunerative white collar jobs usually lived; the Hansons were evidently able to live in a style similar to their neighbors. The Hansons were also prosperous enough to save money for the future purchase of a home, even though the young wife did not work. It was the character of a family life for these proper working class people on which Dreiser focused.[6]

The issue of Hanson's work posed itself between husband and wife in two ways. Since every spare penny was consecrated to savings, any expense the two contemplated for pleasure of their own was the subject of strained discussion. Nothing could go to waste and thus the family did almost nothing outside the everyday routine of the home. There was a subtler tension involved in this frugality as well, for Hanson saw his role in the family as the money maker, and that "contribution" constituted the limits of his authority. He felt inadequate to deal with emotional situations in the family outside the sphere of this contribution. Direction of the family, decisions about its workings, was his wife's job. Yet most of his leisure was spent in the apartment.

Dreiser did not interpret the whole of the family situation in this home in terms of economic restrictions. He saw in the Hansons people who lived an intense family life, apart from the force of their financial limits. Walks in the parks so close at hand, entertaining friends over a cup of coffee in the evenings — these social extensions the family did not permit themselves. Outside of work all human contacts were within the walls of the apartment; in this way their family life was terribly intense. The dullness, the emotional poverty of this family was a part of an isolation of the Hansons from the world around them that Dreiser's heroine, Carrie Meeber, could not endure. Within a short time after she had moved in with her relatives, she left them again to themselves, to their unshakeable routine, to their privacy and intimacy with each other.

Dreiser's portrait of family life bore certain resemblances to the kind of families Wilkie saw in Union Park who were somewhat more affluent. In both pictures, the husbands were no longer the arbiters of family mores and life; they were passive in the home. This was linked in both families to anxieties about status and work; in fact, the husbands' "manliness" was portrayed in both these documents as dependent on what they could achieve in work. The home life in both family pictures was seen to be self-restrictive and intense; men were tied to the home, and yet not leaders there. Social life in the home was sparse, for reasons that could not appear to be explained through simple economics.

Both of these family portraits were thus the mirror opposites of what little Hobart Chatfield-Taylor or Carter Harrison II experienced. Fathers were no longer leaders but rather the supporters of directing mothers; the home had, in some way, become the focus for a new kind of intense family life, a life that was private and isolated. While the older families were home-oriented in their values, they were anything but isolated from others of the same set in Union Park.

Some changes in the institutional structure of Union Park reinforced this new situation within the families.

The Collapse of Multiple Primary Groups

In the pre–Civil War era, the society of the little band of people living near the West Side parks was amiable and intimate, focusing on a diversity of person-to-person contacts. In the middle class era after the Fire, this situation changed in two ways. First the shift in authority between men and women in the family was mirrored in a change in participants in community life. The men were no longer the church leaders, for example; this activity had been taken over by the women. The men now became the passive witnesses of community life, and their forms of recreation, on Wilke's account, were personal and asocial. Secondly, the sheer increase of numbers in the community destroyed the capacity the neighborhood once had for social gatherings in the home. The arena of social contacts had shifted by 1880 to the churches, a more functional, more impersonal, meeting ground, especially since the churches themselves had by 1880 become so large.

This impersonality is evident also in civic responsibilities. The solidly middle class people of this community were reported as "immensely philanthropic," but the terms of philanthropy had changed.[7] Some of the older person-to-person philanthropies left Union Park to follow the wealthy leaders of Chicago in their move to the near North Side. For those enterprises that stayed, like the Washingtonian Home for Female Inebriates, the old patterns of personal visits were discontinued; the institutions had grown too large, and the new patrons did not feel secure enough in their status as models or leaders. This was a part of the same feeling of shame Wilkie noted in the "pretentiousness" of the West Side women. Formal and organized meetings became the means by which social welfare was administered; an impersonal routine in charity was most comfortable for the new generation of Union Park.

It should be said that in the new centers of fashion along the lake much social life was moving out of the home, and into the hotels and clubs in the city's center; such institutions as the New Year's Day visits, the height of the old social season, died out in the decade of the 1880's in Chicago. But the parties given in the Palmer House or in the new Art Institute were still sponsored by a private individual or group of individuals, and the invitations extended on a personal basis.[8]

A church social, or a meeting of a charitable association, could not be run quite the same way. It was difficult to tell people one did not like or, worse, did not know that they could not come to a church dance, or work with one for a good cause. Given the access to all of a church or charity, it must have been hard for the "good works" activities of the West Side to possess the same sense of solidarity and closeness as a dance given in the Union Club ballroom. If the women of Union Park were ashamed of their class position, contrasts of their lot to the "exclusiveness" of the rich may have rankled even more because their own communal institutions were unsuited to exclusion of anyone of a lesser status than themselves. On the other hand, active participation in those communal activities must have had some socio-economic limits, no matter what the leaders thought of the cross they had to bear. The church councilwomen and the patrons of the Washingtonian Home or the lying-in hospital were certainly not drawn primarily from the ranks of the clerical workers or shop assistants who now were coming to live in Union Park. For those at the bottom of the white collar scale, and for the blue collar laborers of the community, one can imagine attendance at some dances or an occasional contribution, enough to be painfully visible to those above, but it is difficult to imagine these "little people" possessing enough leisure or status to be invited to take a directing hand in the church or charity.

For lower white collar groups, there was little else to do in Union Park. There were not many bars and restaurants, because not many people were interested in going out. Fraternal orders had few members from this area, as far as can be determined. The exotica of the ghetto was not found here; pool halls, gambling rooms, a "wild" place like Madame Zulem's Tea and Coffee House, were not right around the corner, but concentrated next to and across the river. If one did not go to church, and if one's wife permitted, an occasional trip to a distant saloon might be the extent of a man's social life.[9]

The change in authority of husbands and the increased family intensity, coupled with this decline of diverse primary-group associations in Union Park, made the isolated family group the encompassing medium of face-to-face relations in the community. It was the family that was the center of companionship as well as nurture; affiliations with peers in other communal structures had grown weak during these middle class years. The family group, documents of the time suggested, was perhaps the only sphere of interpersonal engagement men wanted, and certainly the only coherent sphere they had. "Little islands of propriety," Dreiser called them, little islands in the midst of an enormous city.

Thus the family must be the focus of any attempt to understand how these middle class people forged their relations with the growing city in which they lived; more particularly the patterns of authority within these homes created a special emotional framework for the success or failure men had in the city at large. The family had become *the* medium for interpersonal expression.

It might be thought perhaps that personal relationships were established through wider city contacts, that the community is too narrow a focus for looking at primary-group affiliations. Indeed, a modern school of thought in urban studies led by Scott Greer argues that exactly such contacts appear in cities, despite the accepted notions of the impersonality and anomie of city life.[10] The argument advanced here is not that middle class people like the Union Park men became rootless in the city, but that their roots polarized into a specific channel: the family. Further, the peculiar character of these families as intense and inward-turning groups, as shall be shown, made it likely that whatever other strong social contacts existed ought to have been manifested, if at all, at the local, neighborhood level.

The history of Union Park thus demands a deeper probing of the family group: the middle class families of this community in the years after the Civil War were radically different in structure and tone from the wealthier families of an earlier time for reasons not at all clear from the contemporary sources. But I think it might be useful for the reader, before making further exploration of the conditions of these middle class homes, to see how long the modest homes endured in Union Park's history. What block in time did these families occupy?

Afterword: The Decline of Union Park's Middle Class

Dramatic events had precipitated the sudden arrival of middle class families in Union Park; their exodus from this section of Chicago was a gradual process of slipping away that occurred throughout the whole of the 1890's. Yet the middle classes had deserted the community by the turn of the century, so that the terms of any further study are of a family process spreading across two generations. Three events occurring in 1890 paved the way for the final clearing of respectable people from the area.

The first was the decision of the board of directors of the Chicago World's Fair to locate the Fair at a site on the lakefront rather than near Union Park.[11] The importance of the Fair to the place in which it would be located was obvious: city resources would be concentrated on beautify-

ing the area, an increase in communal publicity and pres-
tige would occur by association with such an exciting event,
an immediate increase in property values and business conducted could also be expected in the locality's stores. This
could have been a chance for Union Park to regain its foot-
ing in the city, but the natural advantage of Lake Michigan prevailed.

The second event of 1890 that was to shape Union Park's
future in the next decade was the adoption by the City
Council of a plan for a Lake Street Elevated Railroad, the
first branch of what is now called the "El" in Chicago, to
run straight west on Lake Street through Union Park, with
stops every quarter mile.[12] The project clearly threatened
property, particularly residential property, along the route.
Moreover, the nature of the new service, which would eventually replace horse-drawn vehicles, meant that Union Park
had less convenient access to transportation than it had
ever known, and transportation of a particularly noisy and
visually unattractive sort. The calm of the houses surrounding the dreamworld parks was now to be shattered by the
smoke and screeching brakes of steam-driven trains, and if
one looked north from a pagoda or duck pond in Union
Park, there would loom on the horizon the two-story high,
black iron bed on which the trains rumbled to and from
the center of town.

The third event in 1890 that altered the fortunes of
Union Park was the opening of the Cold Storage Exchange
building near Halstead Street.[13] This enormous building,
with giant refrigerated vaults and an indoor exchange area,
permitted regular commodity trading of farmers' produce,
which formerly had to be sold almost immediately on arrival. The Cold Storage Exchange, by its very success,
meant other buildings like it were erected in the immediate area, and larger train facilities were built to accommo-

date this new form of agricultural marketing. The warehouse district thus came to stretch again to Halstead Street, so that the eastern area adjacent to Union Park remained a market center, but under modern conditions of exchange that greatly increased the volume and scope of trade conducted there and passed, in trains and vans, through Union Park.[14]

Thus the old homes and quiet streets lost their primness, and were gradually deserted by "proper" families. In their place came a great polygot foreign colony, where Greeks, Poles, Italians, and Russian Jews crowded together in the now decrepit homes and apartment houses, until the cranes and bulldozers of a massive urban renewal project scattered them a few years ago.

Part Two

THE PATTERNS OF A YEAR

4

UNION PARK'S PLACE IN

A MODERN DEBATE ABOUT FAMILIES

The Unanswered Questions of Union Park's History

The history of this Chicago community contains four puzzles. First, and most striking, is why the structure of authority and influence should have changed in Union Park families from that prevailing in the upper class era before the Civil War to the quite different relations existing during the middle class period of the 1870's and 1880's. For in the early, wealthier period the authority and moral power of the family were clearly focused on the father, and to his judgment the wife and children deferred. In the middle class years of this neighborhood, the roles seem to have been reversed. Women were pictured as the rulers of the family, or at the least as independent of their husbands' will; the men were taken to be passive in decisions of home and immediate community life. The roles of these middle class fathers narrowed to providing the money necessary for the family to live.

Why this shift in control of the family should have occurred is a problem on which contemporary documents were mute. Was this pattern of family life peculiar to the new people as an urban middle class; was it due to some relation the middle class father had to other men in the city different from his earlier, more affluent counterpart's; was it due to changed circumstances in the city at large? To these questions, germane to the substance of the historical development, the extant materials from the nineteenth century tell little in reply.

A second puzzle of family life during the middle class era in Union Park involves the character of the families themselves. They were pictured at the time to be sometimes dull and drab, rather joyless affairs, sometimes unions of great warmth and mutuality. But the families all were marked out for a special "intensity." The history of the community gives a particular meaning to that term. In Union Park there were few bars, few clubs, few restaurants; entertaining friends was considered a rare and special occasion. Women's contacts with each other occurred through church charitable work, but the churches were now grown enormous and less like a little band of worshipers. In place of these wider social circles, the family bounded the social terrain of husband and wife alike. It was to the livingroom armchair rather than the local pub that the middle class fathers of this community repaired after dinner, and if one looked into the busiest streets of the community at night, one saw few people venturing out of their homes. What caused the middle class families to live this way? In the richer and in the poorer sections of Chicago, such isolation was not remarked by contemporaries; in fact the opposite was true, for observers noted how much time both rich and poor spent, socially, outside the circle of their family lives.

A third major question is related to this isolation and privacy of Union Park families and the patterns of authority within the home. What were the conditions of child

nurturing that these intense, mother-oriented homes produced? What was it like for a little boy or girl to grow up
in such a sedate part of the big city, far from the glitter of
the center of town, or from the disorganized chaos of the
slums, but far also from the excitement that was a part of
these other places? Something of the rigidities of school
life in Union Park at the time is known, but little of the
discipline of the home.

Finally, there is the question of how employment was
related to these family conditions in Union Park. For between husbands and wives, whether at the richer or the
poorer end of the social spectrum, there seemed a particular marital tension over the issue of work; how was such a
tension related to the balance of power between men and
women in the home? The question poses itself again in
terms of the isolation and intensity of these homes; what
relation did this isolation bear to the work experience of
people in Union Park families? Most significantly, and perhaps the most puzzling problem of all, was the relation between experience of work and the raising of children. Men
attempt to pass on the lessons of their lives to those whom
they have created and nurtured. In these intense, isolated
families, the transmission of worldly knowledge, gained
from work, to the young must have had a special quality;
the extant documents raise the problem but offer little in
the way of a solution.

The broader framework for understanding these puzzles
is to be found in a theoretical debate now current between
a prominent American sociologist and a French cultural
historian, a debate concerning the changed structure of
families under preindustrial and industrial conditions. To
this larger debate, the unresolved questions of Union
Park's history speak, and, in turn, the issues of the debate

illuminate the conditions of family, and the relation of family to work, in this middle class community of Chicago's industrial era.

The Debate over "Intense" Urban Families

The American sociologist Talcott Parsons and the French historian Phillippe Ariès have both sought to describe a pattern of family life they regard as unique to the industrial world and its cities:[1] a small, private family of father, mother, and their children, without other relatives living in the house, and without close obligations and ties to relatives who live nearby. Both define this kind of family as "nuclear," the anthropological term for a family composed of a conjugal pair and their offspring. But the kind of family Parsons and Ariès are at pains to understand derives its character not only from the composition of the kin members, but from its small size, its restricted or weak allegiance to relatives, the lack of privacy and separateness within the family group itself. Their intent is thus to describe a cluster of conditions pervading a private and intense family existence, though they label these families of the modern, nonagrarian, industrial age by their structure alone.

Both men believe the nuclear family to be the dominant order of the industrial era, but for opposing reasons, and with a divergent sense of its value and worth. What each of these writers seeks is some way to understand how intense and private family life might be related to the acculturation of the child and his training for assuming his own tasks later in life, in work or in his own family responsibilities. The theories of Ariès and Parsons suggest in fact two radically different directions that this family form could provide for the young who were to be led from the home out into the work world of the city, and it is in the attempt to understand the preparation in the family for the larger social order that these writers come most directly into conflict.

Ariès' definition of a "modern, nuclear" family, a family form he believes dominant since the opening of the industrial era, is very similar to the kind of families that were to be found in the Union Park section of Chicago: a conjugal pair and their children living in a polarized situation, where the father represented the family in the work world at large, where the mother did not work, and the children were trained for more than a decade in the schools, until they entered the work world at the end of adolescence. Each of the members had a functional place in the family, and the functions did not overlap.

This kind of family Ariès believes to be in sharp contrast to the families of the preindustrial order. In the medieval period, Ariès' researches led him to conclude, the length of time that men were considered children was much shorter than the period we now call childhood. After the age of seven or eight, a man was treated as an incipient adult, with the same powers of understanding and feeling as people three or four times his age; in other words, a human being was allotted a shorter period of time in which he was considered helpless in the world, and at what seems to us an impossibly early age was expected to function with much the same feeling and sense of values as his parents.

This condition of a short period of helplessness in the world, defined as childhood, Ariès associates with family conditions where kin members outside the conjugal pair and their children were usually an intimate part of the family group. A wide range of kin lived closely intermixed, so that the sense of the privacy and separateness of the conjugal group was not felt; Ariès links the spatial organization of the house itself to this diversification, for the rooms of the medieval houses were not specialized in function; the same room could serve as dining hall, sitting room, and bedroom.

Ariès sets himself a broader task than to reveal simply an earlier era's different conception of manhood and the boundaries of the home circle. From his generalized picture of the past, he seeks to jolt the reader to understand what is distinctive and peculiar about the present. In the family emerging into the industrial era, Ariès argues, the length of time a person was considered to be a helpless being extended to almost a third of his life span. And being helpless, and so unlike his parents, he required a great deal of training to be able to function in the adult world. Thus he was forced to go to school for a much longer time, and receive training of a sort unlike what would be appropriate for those different creatures called adults.

But the prolonged period of helplessness, the increase in the stage of life called childhood, was concomitant, Ariès shows, with the development of the sense of a private family, limited to the conjugal pair and their offspring. It is unclear in Ariès' work whether or not this form of family arose because of the growing need to shelter helpless children, though the isolated conditions of the nuclear family would presumably serve as a better means of control and training than an amorphous, diverse household. At one point in his work Ariès relates this functional specialization of the family to the growing division of labor in society, but not much is made of the point. Seemingly, the nuclear family developed out of an internal, historical dialogue between the growth of the concept of helpless childhood and the growth of a belief in the intimacy of the conjugal household as a virtue.

Ariès has the integrity to make a moral judgment about

his historical materials, a judgment sharply critical of the limitations of the "nuclear" or "intensive" family on the growth of the members within it. As a result of the growth of privacy in the family, and the rationale of better training of the young in a more isolated, controlled setting, Ariès argues, the intensive family of the industrial era cast the members of the home who did not work into a retreat from the world at large; the head of the family was expected to represent and protect the home in the world, the wife and the children to live apart from the world and the temptations to be found in it. Thus the division of labor in the family would compound the sense of isolation that the family created for itself in order to shield those helpless beings within it, the children. The outcome of this situation was that the children growing up in such homes were deprived of much experience of the adult world that they could have used, and they had a greater difficulty, in Ariès' view, of becoming responsible, knowing actors in society than did children in the older tradition. In this way, the combination of a concept of helpless children who must be nurtured and trained for a long time, the concept of the virtue of privacy in the family, and the division of labor in the family vitiated the depth of experience of young people raised in this family form. This historical confluence denied young people a chance to create a fund of experience with, and judgment about, other people. Presumably this ineptitude would reflect itself when the young went out in the world, to work or to marry.

In Ariès' critique, then, the movement from the diverse family system of the ancien régime to the private, functionalized, sheltered nuclear family system of the industrial era changed the way in which the developing children and adolescents were socialized to the world around them. The change in family structure was, on his account, the growth of a barrier for the child to overcome as he learned to deal with the society in which he lived.

The implications of Ariès' ideas come into sharp focus only when set against the alternative explanation for the same family phenomena to be found in the writings of Talcott Parsons.

As was true for his master, Max Weber, Parsons' neutral and descriptive language hides within it a host of assumed values and judgments of what is socially "good"; one of the great virtues of Ariès' work is to show us to what degree Parsons' descriptions of the function of the family are actually "ideal" descriptions in a value sense as well as in a Weberian, ideal-typical sense.

The vices of the modern nuclear family for Ariès are, to a great extent, its virtues for Parsons. Where Ariès sees the specialization of the family as a limitation on human capacities to grow, Parsons sees this specialization as both a necessary consequence of the increasing specialization of the whole society, and as a means of leading the child step by step into a position where he could act alone as an adult in a complex industrial world. For Parsons, the fact that the child in an isolated nuclear family would have "farther to go," as he puts it, in becoming an adult than children in another historical era is not an indictment of the family form, but an indicator of the increased complexity of the industrial society, in which the family plays a more specialized role.

This means, concretely, that the emergence from childhood into young adulthood would be a process wherein the young man learned to see how fragmented his power was in the world, and how separate the various spheres of social life were. The isolated family was a medium for accustoming the young to the many nonemotional areas of social activity, held together by functional bonds only. Thus a young person would learn to evaluate himself, as a man and eventually as a husband, in terms of his ability to perform a special task, that is, to act as an economic and social mediator between the shelter of the family and the society at large. Presumably — and the point is logically deducible from Parsons' work, though he does not state it as an explicit assumption — people in an industrial-bureaucratic situation who do not thus learn their functional limits, or the value of self-limitation, will be ultimately disoriented and disfunctional in the work world; those who expect a kind of self-sufficient competence and activity in themselves will be in fact incapable of dealing adequately with a world in which division of labor and specialization are the dominant themes. In cultures like America's, where a premium is put on self-reliance, Parsons expects the ideal to be defeated by the way the bureaucracies of the industrial order function.

Thus, Parsons by implication casts the process of upbringing in the extended family as inhibiting in modern times for exactly those reasons that Ariès sees it as being a form of strength. For Parsons, socialization of the child requires a long period of learning about himself as a fragmented being: Parsons' brilliant perception of this process of learning as a form of ego development brings together the psychoanalytic description of child development with the structural analysis of sociology, for it is the essence of ego formation to learn the proper limits and spheres of action. Ariès, one concludes, although his description is here vague, views a capacity to deal with the work world as involving first and foremost a general understanding of other men; the attack Ariès makes on the intense nuclear family is in terms of what it has done to the child's emotional and moral understanding. As the child matures, Ariès says, he will not have the direct experience of the world of adults gained by being in their company for most of the time, or by being treated like one of them. Here Ariès perceives an irony. The reason for treating children as "pure" or "uncorrupted," when the concept solidified in the nineteenth century, was to prepare and train them to be adults in a corrupted world; yet because of this regimen children were denied the opportunity to learn directly and immediately how to deal with the complexity and the corruption that they might experience in the people around them. The irony of the nuclear family for Parsons is that a man will feel strong, and feel as though he has an identity, only by knowing how to act as a limited creature, by being capable of sustaining and justifying himself in not doing too much.

In Parsons' work, then, is to be found a sweeping, almost global, description of the structures of family such as those in this one Chicago community during the late nineteenth century. On his account, the intense families of Union Park might be interpreted as a sign of the adaptation of these people to the conditions of industrial and bureaucratic growth occurring in large cities at this time. The fathers would have retreated from dominance in the governance of the home, while they remained responsible for the economic support of the family; such a limitation of functions in the family would merely be a sign of the power of the industrial system to create fragmented social relations and division of labor even within the family. Further, Parsons looks on this division as worthwhile, since the experience of fragmentation at home prepares the young for the division and fragmentation they will experience later in all manner of activity during adult lives.

Bridging the History and the Theories

And thus the conditions of family life in this Chicago community come to seem larger in their meaning than the local history of the time and place might suggest. These theories are two poles of understanding that can be applied to frame a deeper enquiry into the family life of the community. But this further enquiry is as well demanded by the theories, for each is predictive, each attempts to describe what power a pattern of historical development in the community — the emergence of private, intense family life — could have had on the chances of success or failure for the families involved. In Ariès' account, the young nurtured under such circumstances should have great difficulty in the world, while in Parsons' theory they should have acquired the capacity to adapt to fragmented conditions of work and future family life in the city. As there comes to be known something more specific about the generations of young people and their parents in this urban community, it should be possible to evaluate the relative merits of these two general theories. I propose to explore these theories not as hypotheses to be mechanically tested, but as two conflicting guides to the experience of a particular group of families.

Social theories tend to lose some of their satisfying logical rigor when related to concrete historical circumstances, for the lines of the theories come to be absorbed and transformed by the uniqueness inherent in all historical events. Union Park's special setting as a "first-generation" middle class community in a rapidly expanding city casts a new perspective in which the theories of Parsons and Ariès can be judged. For these theories touch only in generalities on the puzzling phenomena revealed in the documentary history of this community; to make a more inclusive explanation, it will be necessary to try to understand what such families experienced during an era of rapid urban change, and how these urban changes affect the most intimate patterns of Union Park life.

The lives of the Union Park people must be explored both within the family circle and in terms of what the family members did in the city to sustain themselves. Each of the theories attempts to show what the quality of the family life will do to the young when cast as an adult into the world on his own.

The nature of the family group, and its relation to work, are themes of social life portrayed in the following pages in an unusual way. The means of this further study are statistical ones, not because numbers are somehow "better" guides than contemporary words, but because certain statistical documents available for this community offer a unique opportunity to evaluate these themes of family experience.

Handwritten manuscripts for the U.S. Census provide an extensive look into the conditions of work and family life in Union Park during one year, 1880, at the height of the middle class era; tracing fathers and sons through city directories, back almost a decade and forward a decade, probes the experience of success and failure in work among two generations of the family.

It may appear at first that statistics would be ill-suited guides in this enterprise: what, after all, are the statistics of privacy, what numbers describe the intimacy of a family, or, for that matter, its success or failure in the world? Clearly, the first task is to determine where, if at all, quantitative measures of a community intersect with qualitative ones; it is a question of determining what in the demography of Union Park bears on its history and on the conflicting theories which frame that history.

5

ELEMENTARY CONDITIONS

OF FAMILY AND LABOR

In 1880, census takers found 12,000 people living in the forty blocks of Union Park which map our study. The census takers classed these 12,000 people into units they called "households" — a household being any distinct residence, from that of a single person to a mansion with many servants. The statistics on people were taken individually, yet every individual was placed within this kind of residential frame. The system was a simple one; for the qualitative questions we want to ask of these statistics, it was too simple. What kinds of families created these households, what were the structures that brought people to live together?

The Family Structures of Union Park

Families can be sorted easily in two ways: by the kind and the number of people living together. This is a common division in anthropological work, and it is useful to us in tracing the development of an intense, private family life within the households of Union Park. Writers like Parsons and Ariès single out the form of family organization during the industrial urban era as specially intense and private; the number of people in a home should also have affected the quality of privacy and the degree to which the family could be controlled by its leaders.

THE KINSHIP STRUCTURE. The nuclear family, as the term is used by Parsons, Ariès, and most other modern writers, refers to a family in which a husband and wife live alone with their growing children. These nuclear families, supposedly intense homes, dominated Union Park but were not the only kinds of kinship structure to be found there. In addition, there existed families that were simply single persons living alone, usually termed single-member families, and families of a more complicated structure, called extended families. In extended families, the kinship system included any of the relatives excluded from the nuclear group. Such a family might contain an old man no longer able to work who had gone to live with his children, or two spinster sisters living together, or a family that had taken in a country cousin for the year. All three family structures, single member, nuclear, and extended, could in the census classification be a household with nonrelatives as well, boarders and servants who lived in the home, for instance. These nonrelatives are commonly termed "satellites" to each of the structures of kinship. The great majority of households in Union Park were without satellites; they were simple families in the usual sense of the word.

In Union Park, the bulk of the population lived in families of the nuclear form. Table 2 shows the statistics for this pattern. It might be thought that boarders and servants would have been unevenly distributed in the three kinds of families, that single-member families, for example, would have few instances of servant or boarder satellites. This did not occur. The apportioning of the community into four fifths nuclear, one tenth single-member, and one tenth extended families held when the satellites were removed from consideration and only the bonds between related people considered.

Table 2. Distribution of people into three family structures, Union Park

Type of family	Number of members	Percentage of community
Nuclear	9,731	81.1
Extended	1,186	9.9
Single-member	1,087	9.9
Total	12,004	100

If private and intense families were the product, as Ariès and Parsons both believe, of a nuclear form of family structure, here certainly would be a statistical base for their arguments, for the kinship system was overwhelmingly nuclear in Union Park. Yet Union Park was at this time a middle class area; the question naturally comes to mind as to whether such nuclear-family dominance is a middle class trait. In her pioneering study of Irish workers in London, Lynn Lees discovered the same pattern of nuclear dominance of family life, to the very proportions found in Union Park, in a poor community of London whose wretchedness and raucous street life made it as far from the respectably sedate homes of Union Park as can be imagined.[1] A demographic structure more complicated than the mere dominance in numbers of nuclear families in Union Park evidently was involved in creating the sedate privacy of these middle class homes. One pertinent factor is the ages of people in nuclear families when compared to profiles of other family types.

In Union Park, there were almost no young children abandoned by their parents and living alone as street urchins; the 1880 census takers could find only ten such single-member families. Whether this was actually a high or low number compared to a poorer community we can only guess. Victor Hugo's earlier picture in *Les Miserables* of the *gamins,* or lone street children of Paris, suggests their numbers to have been large in the poor Parisian section he described, but certainly no reliable, statistical information is available for nineteenth-century European or American cities.

The childhood population of the nuclear and extended families in Union Park diverged somewhat. In those nuclear families, without boarders or servants, 27.2 percent of the family population was composed of children under fifteen. In similar extended families, 18.4 percent were under fifteen. The nuclear homes contained, similarly, a larger proportion of teenagers from fifteen to nineteen years old.

Thus a slightly larger proportion of children marked the nuclear homes of Union Park than the extended ones, and conversely the extended homes contained a greater percentage of adults. But it was within the adult group itself that age differences between the single-member, nuclear, and extended families of Union Park were sharpest.

Nearly half of the single-member families during 1880 were composed of young people between the ages of twenty-one and thirty; this concentration was about 20 percent more than that of young adults living in nuclear or extended family relationships during this year. There were, on the other hand, relatively few people between the ages of thirty and fifty living alone; of those people in later middle age and old age, there were again a fair percentage living alone, mostly widows and widowers.

The differences between the ages of adults in nuclear and extended families were a little more complicated. Husbands and wives in nuclear families were very similar in their age groupings to husbands and wives in extended families. Both family types were composed of spouses whose ages were rather evenly spread from twenty-five to fifty. But there was a tendency for the family members outside the conjugal pair in extended households to be older than the wives in these households, so that the outsider, unlike Dreiser's Carrie Meeber, was not a youngster, but someone in his or her late thirties or forties. These outsiders had as well a special marital character.

Table 3 shows the marital status of the family members in nuclear and extended homes. In the groups over thirty, it is clear that the extended families contained proportionately many more unmarried people than the nuclear families. The reason for this was that, in extended family homes, the "extra" kin member was likely to be an unmarried adult; there were few related, married couples living together as an extended family, though scattered groups of unmarried sisters, brothers, or cousins shared quarters. In all, 72 percent of the extended families were composed of married couples who had taken in an unmarried, mature adult relative; this situation is commonly defined as the existence of collateral kin creating an extended family, though the term collateral kin at its broadest can include both married and unmarried relatives.[2]

It is the maiden aunt or cousin, not the little girl with wanderlust, who had typically joined these Union Park homes. This condition suggests a family structure nearer to that conceived by Ariès as "extended," where multiplicity of adults might be present who could have acted as parents to the children, where the polarity of father-worker, mother-parent was weakened by the presence of fully mature relatives. Thus not only did the families of Union Park evince a dominant group of families whose nuclear structure was related to the debate between Parsons and

Table 3. Marital status of people in nuclear and extended families, in age categories from 25 to 55[a]

| | People from 25–29 | | People from 30–34 | | People from 35–39 | |
	Nuclear	Extended	Nuclear	Extended	Nuclear	Extended
Single	18.7%	56.0%	7.9%	42.0%	3.7%	35.6%
Married	78.3	38.7	88.6	52.2	90.7	60.0
Widowed	2.4	4.0	3.3	4.3	4.5	2.2
Divorced[b]	0.5	1.3	0.2	1.4	1.0	2.2
Total	100	100	100	100	100	100
	N = 576	N = 75	N = 508	N = 69	N = 484	N = 45

| | People from 40–44 | | People from 45–49 | | People from 50–54 | |
	Nuclear	Extended	Nuclear	Extended	Nuclear	Extended
Single	2.6%	11.1%	2.1%	31.6%	2.5%	15.0%
Married	90.9	74.1	87.9	52.6	81.9	45.0
Widowed	6.3	14.8	10.0	15.8	14.7	40.0
Divorced[b]	0.3	0.0	0.0	0.0	1.0	0.0
Total	100	100	100	100	100	100
	N = 350	N = 27	N = 240	N = 19	N = 204	N = 20

[a] In homes without boarders or servants.
[b] This category is misleading, and will be examined later in the study.

Ariès, but an alternative family mode as well, comprising about 1200 people, or a tenth of the community, with certain similarities to the family type Ariès describes for an earlier era.

There is of course a question as to how long such families as these extended ones endured. Short-lived extended family relations have been thought to be one medium through which migration to cities was accomplished at this time; a young newcomer to the city went to live temporarily with a relative until a home of his or her own could be created. In literature, *Sister Carrie* or Frank Lloyd Wright's *Autobiography* show such temporary family extension, involved in the migration to Chicago of young people starting out in life. The age structure of extended families in Union Park suggests that in this community the bulk of extended families did not fit this picture. In addition, further study of the families in Union Park, which will show an enormous difference between the mobility of nuclear and extended families, the residential patterns of the two family forms, and the relations between the generations, suggests that family extension in this community was of such a duration, or had such an impact, that strong marks were left on the family as a whole. How this marking took place shall constitute a major theme of our study.

FAMILY SIZE AND STRUCTURE. For the householders of Union Park, the number of people in their families was not an abstract sociological factor, but a real and immediate cause for concern. Unlike the situation in the older farm communities, where each person in the family was expected to work, and where the advent of children was a future economic boon as well as an immediate emotional one, the larger the family in an urban area, the more the economic drain on that family's resources. Each new child was an additional expense, and since Union Park children did not work until late adolescence, the child himself would not be a contributor to the family's income until he was almost ready to leave it.

Allied to this economic burden was the fact that the men and women of this nineteenth century community had no real means of controlling the size of their families, other than through abstinence. The technology of birth control was at best primitive, and, as we shall see in the next chapter, the available technology was not used without a feeling of shame, if it was employed at all. Emotional fear and economic threat combined to make a powerful bond of repression for the men and women of that time. The data on Union Park show, however, that this repression worked: families were able to limit themselves to a small, intimate size.

Table 4. Family size in Union Park in 1880

Number of kin members	Number of families in this category	Percentage of total number of families in Union Park	Number of people in this category
1	833	27.4	883
2	763	23.7	1526
3	570	17.7	1710
4	369	11.5	1476
5	289	9.0	1445
6	162	5.0	972
7	77	2.4	539
8	59	1.8	472
9	25	0.8	225
10	23	0.7	230

Table 4 shows the pattern of this limitation. Clearly the number of families decreased as the size of the family measured became larger. On the other hand, the number of individual people represented under each of these divisions did not decrease in this direct way. The 883 single-member families represented 883 people; the 369 families with four kinship members represented 1476 individuals. In terms of the numbers of people represented, the bulk of the Union Park population was from families with two to six family members.

In this, the families of Union Park in Chicago differed little from what is known about families in other cities at the time. The Union Park families were similar in profile to those of Brooklyn in 1890 — then solidly middle class — and to middle class families of Boston in 1880.[3] Surprisingly, the profile of family size in Union Park was also very similar to that of a poor Negro community in Philadelphia and to poorer white communities in Chicago itself. Differences in family size seem in fact to have depended at this time more on the rural or urban location of a family — if it was urban it tended to be smaller — than on a family's class character within the city.[4]

A family with one child was a different affair, however, than a family with three or four children. The burden of support, economically, was greater in a somewhat large home, and the emotional "clinch" between parent and child, as Erikson calls it, was weaker when parents had to divide their time and affection among children at different stages of growth.

The differences in family size between nuclear and extended families are shown in Table 5. Clearly, the nuclear families were more concentrated at the minimal family size of two people. This occurred in part because there were more young people recently married in the nuclear families than pairs of spinsters or cousins living together in the extended families. Significantly, Table 5 shows extended families to have had a somewhat higher concentration than

Table 5. Sizes of nuclear and extended families[a]

Number of family members	Family type	
	Nuclear	Extended
2	41%	28%
3	24	30
4	13	19
5	10	10
6	6	6
7	3	2
Total	97[b]	95[b]
	100% N = 4831	100% N = 549

[a] Without boarders or servants.
[b] The remainder lived in families of from 8 to 20 people.

nuclear ones at the level of three or four family members, but not at larger levels. As the census manuscripts reveal, the extended families of three and four were composed either of a man and wife with some additional relative in the house, or man, wife, and small child, with an extra relative. At the level of five or six family members, there appeared similarly to be a relative or two attached to a "regular" family grouping of husband, wife, and, at most, two children. Large groups of kin unmarried to each other, like three brothers, or widowed in-laws, were rare.

The stereotype of the extended family on the farm, in which ten or twelve people sat down to table together and worked in the fields together, did not fit the conditions of extended families in this Chicago community. The urban extended families were a little larger, but not much.

We are accustomed to think that a family with one child will lead to a more intensive relationship between parent and child than a family with four children, the supply of human energy and affection not being infinitely expandable. But it has been common in the literature on family life to link this intensity due to small family size to the emergence, historically, of the nuclear family as the dominant mode of organization; such is Parsons' idea, for instance. In Union Park at this time, the dependence of family size on family form did not occur. Size was an independent, though interacting, element apart from family form in creating the character of home life in this community.

ETHNICITY AND FAMILY STRUCTURE. "Ethnicity" is a term of social description that has no meaning apart from the historical conditions in which it occurs. The Pilgrims who migrated to America in the seventeenth century were obviously "immigrants" in a much different way than the Polish peasants who migrated to New York at the turn of the present century; they had a different set of power relationships to the "natives," a different set of notions about assimilation, and so on.

In Chicago at the opening of the 1880's, as elsewhere in America, the influx of immigrants from Southern and Eastern Europe had only just begun. Migration was still largely from common-language countries like England, Scotland, and Canada, and those immigrants from countries of a different language were not uniformly cast as outsiders who were less desirable than natives. Germans in America, for example, were relatively easily assimilated, though English-speaking Irish faced a much more difficult time. Simplistic, rigid sanctions of the insiders against the outsiders did not prevail; the discrimination was selective. In Union Park, ethnicity was an even more subtle condition, for this respectable area attracted the prosperous foreigner more than it did the disadvantaged one. There were in Union Park, as was shown in Chapter Three, much lower concentrations of Irish, Scandinavians, and French Canadians — the three foreign groups suffering the most obvious hardships at this time — than in Chicago as a whole.

The Census of 1880 showed 11.1 percent of the foreign-born to live in single-member families, compared to 8.3 percent of the native-born living alone; 11.4 percent of the foreign-born in extended families, compared to 9.5 percent of the native-born; the remainder of both foreign- and native-born living in nuclear families. There was then a very slight tendency for the foreign-born as a whole to occupy the minority family types. It certainly could not be said that foreigners huddled together in extended family units, or drifted alone, and the natives inhabited the dominant family form, the nuclear unit. If only adults in the community be considered, family differences between native-born and foreign-born were virtually nonexistent in 1880. Stereotypes of the immigrant family sheltering assorted grandfathers, uncles, and cousins do not fit the way these residents of Union Park lived.

Migrants from different regions of America were almost entirely uniform in their family structure; among the people who came to Chicago from New England, for instance, there were to be found the same concentrations of single-member, nuclear, and extended families living in Union Park during this year as in the group who came from the Old South.

People from the different European countries showed the same distribution into single-member and extended families, with a few minor exceptions, as did the American-born families. The only differences among the foreign groups came within the nuclear family pattern itself; the differences were in how boarders or servants were attached to the basic nuclear unit. Irish and Canadians were very likely to live in nuclear homes as satellites, the first as servants, the second as boarders. In the other family groupings of extended or single-member families, Irish and Canadians did not evince this trend.

In general, there was an enormous unity between people of various ethnic backgrounds in their family patterns. This unity poses its own question: why should birthplace have counted for so little in the lives of these people?

As noted before, the 1880 Census revealed the absence of an immigrant ghetto in Union Park at this time, and the presence of integrated living arrangements. The great similarity between native and foreign families may have been one reason why this residential integration was possible. That is, it might have been hard for ethnic groups to band together by virtue of their foreignness if they themselves did not possess, in common, special family qualities. It seems logical that configurations of the family would act as integrating agents between native and foreigner, and the fact of ethnicity would take a secondary role in shaping communal associations.

The relation of foreign birth to family size in Union Park was also a part of this condition, for here too was a similarity to be found between foreigner and native families. Immigrants from the various countries of Europe were little different from Union Park citizens born in the United States in size of family, all families being predominantly from 2 to 6 people. There was some tendency for German families to be a little larger than the average, and for Irish families to be a little smaller, but the differences were not great. In family size, as in family form, it seems reasonable that the structure of the family provided a bond across whatever differences might have been felt between the native and the foreign born; in this way, family structure may have permitted residential integration to become a reality for these middle class people.

The Conditions of Working Life

Today the lines between social class and occupation are blurred. An unskilled factory operative can earn as much as a school teacher; a lawyer can earn a princely income every year or barely enough to support his family. In addition, styles of expenditures and consumption have come to cut across class lines, so that the possessions and activities of a family are not a reliable guide to its economic position.

The situation in nineteenth century Chicago was clearer, for there existed at that period direct connections between the kind of work performed and the income level of a worker. The economic difference between forms of work was simple, even brutal: a white collar worker made about twice what a skilled laborer made, and as much as three times the earnings of an unskilled operative. The economic base of a family was thus more clearly seen in the kind of work the wage-earner engaged in.

The Census of 1880 did not, unfortunately, ask for the income of each household, so that no unique information on income in Union Park in 1880 is available. A wage scale for the city as a whole was made in the next Census, however, and it can be assumed that professionals, factory workers, or clerks in Union Park did not differ substantially in income from similar workers in other parts of the city. The 1890 Census portrayed the differences of income between white and blue collar workers shown in Table 6.

Here is how that income was spent. For a family earning $840 but saving every penny they could, expenditures were, on one account: rent, $200; food, $260; fuel, $50; clothing, $25; amusements, $15. Thus about $290 could be saved. For a richer family keeping a servant, with two children,

Table 6. Average Chicago annual wage, 1890, in major industries

	Average annual wage
All employees in manufacturing	$ 590.23
Officers, firm members, and clerks	
Males over 16 years	1,006.25[a]
Females over 15 years	531.16
Operatives, skilled and unskilled	
Males over 16 years	587.14
Females over 15 years	313.26
Children	184.12
Pieceworkers	
Males over 16 years of age	574.29
Females over 15 years	299.39
Children	221.60

[a] The number of clerks in the first category is overwhelmingly larger than the number of executives, and so wages are probably scaled down, not inflated abnormally.

on an income of $1100 a year, expenses followed this pattern: rent, $300; food, $420; fuel, $60; clothing, $50; amusements, $20; sickness, $5; travel and servant, $150.[5] The major differences between these two budgets, the first that of a prosperous working class family, the second of a white collar family, were in expenses for clothing, rent, and food. Affluence did not bring an increase in the amount spent on amusements or entertainment. In fact, the family living on $550 spent almost the same on amusements as the family living on double that salary.

In the ranks of manual labor itself, level of skill in a job seemed to affect sharply the amount of pay a worker would receive. A worker in meatpacking, then a semiskilled craft, earned about $450; an unskilled worker in a sweatshop received between $200 and $240.[6] Because the differences were so sharp between white collar and blue collar, and within the blue collar classes themselves, the occupation of workers in Union Park thus was critical in determining their affluence and standing in the community.

The spread of occupations in Union Park indicates the status of the workers of this community in two ways: first, through the relation of groups of workers to each other within Union Park, and, second, through the relation of the majority of these workers to the labor structure of Chicago as a whole.

Table 7 shows the distribution of jobs within Union Park. Of those who worked, the Census showed 62 percent to be white collar workers, 26 percent skilled or unskilled blue collar workers, and 16 percent servants. Most of the

Table 7. The structure of occupations in Union Park

Occupational group	Number	Percentage
White collar		
Business executives	270	7
Professionals	339	5
Artists	158	3
Proprietors of stores	552	9
Clerical employees	1,299	22
Commercial service (bakers, saloon keepers, traveling salesmen, tailors)	939	16
Blue collar		
Manual workers, highly skilled	181	3
Manual workers, skilled	559	9
Manual workers, semiskilled	318	6
Manual workers, unskilled	205	3
Transport workers[a]	299	5
Servants		
All domestic servants	943	16

[a] Business and government employees (telegraph company, street railway company, railroads, and so forth) who list the utility they work for as their job. Almost all of these workers are involved in the communication-transport nexus of the city. There is certainly some error in the ascription of *all* transport employees to blue collar status. The census error here is not remediable.

servants were attached to the homes of the wealthier people of the community. But, wealthy or not, the bulk of the working population did not perform manual or industrial labor.

It is tempting to assume these figures speak for themselves, yet if 80 percent of the working people in Chicago were white collar, Union Park might well have been thought to be depressed or poor. In fact, however, Union Park's workers were favorably situated in the job structure of Chicago, as shown in Table 8.[7] Clearly, the occupational pattern in Union Park did not resemble Chicago as a whole during this year; at the more skilled levels of manual labor, in the professions, in executive and proprietary positions, and especially in clerical work, Union Park was more concentrated than the city as a whole. Conversely, Union Park contained disproportionately few unskilled factory laborers. The fact that the community possessed many more servants, most of whom were residential, again indicated a pattern of affluence different from that of the city in aggregate.

The comfortable position of the majority of workers in Union Park did not depend on peculiarities in the work force of Chcago at this time. Union Park's job structure was just as favorable in comparison to general labor conditions in Boston in 1880; a long established poor community of blacks in Philadelphia at the other end of the economic scale showed patterns of jobholding directly opposed to the patterns of this white, native-born neighborhood.[8]

Table 8 shows also that workers from Union Park encountered in Chicago an economic order much different from the Pennsylvania coal towns, the Ohio steel centers, or the New England mill centers of the time. Chicago's job structure was not monolithically centered around meatpacking or garment-making, around rails or shipping;

Table 8. Percentage of work force in selected occupations, Union Park compared to Chicago as a whole, 1880

	Union Park	Chicago	Index of difference[a] (100 = same percentage distribution)
Professionals			
Lawyers	1.16%	.54%	214
Teachers	1.51	.78	193
Doctors	1.24	.47	263
Executives			
Bankers	.32	.34	94
Real estate and insurance	2.58	1.79[b]	144
Officials of manufacturing concerns	.75	.58	129
Artists and art teachers	2.58	.56[b]	460
Proprietors	9.01	5.79	155
Clerical			
Clerks, general	5.32	.46	1,156
Clerks and bookkeepers in manufacturing establishment	3.80	.12	3,166
Clerk, salesman, or accountant in store	10.80	7.92	136
Commercial service			
Commercial travelers	2.25	1.42	158
Nonfactory tailor, dressmaker, or milliner	7.22	8.47	85
Manual highly skilled			
Printer	2.32	1.55	149
Manual skilled			
Carpenter	2.89	3.54	81
Machinist	2.27	1.47	154
Manual semiskilled			
Boot and shoe makers	.81	1.18	68
Butchers	.60	1.41	42
Painters or varnishers	1.81	2.12	85
Manual unskilled			
Unspecified day laborers	1.79	12.87	19
Mill or factory operatives	.96	.90	105
Domestic servants	15.40	7.60	202

[a] Computed $100 \times \dfrac{\text{percent in Union Park}}{\text{percent in Chicago}}$.

[b] Figure for 1890; 1880 figure not available.

the city was too complex. It was a rail center, and a stock-yard center, and a garment center all at once. Even compared to Berlin, a European city with a comparably phenomenal rate of economic growth in the last third of the nineteenth century, Chicago's job structure was specially diverse.[9]

The question naturally arises as to how the white collar workers of a community like Union Park dealt with such economic diversity. While these middle class people were by no means rich, they were placed as a group more favorably in the city than the common run of workers; the spread of occupations in the city, the richness of enterprise, was to expand continually throughout the end of the nineteenth century in Chicago, and open up ever new opportunities in white collar as well as industrial work.

The diversified vigor of the city was, in fact, the social framework that made questions about the training of children specially relevant. For on one theoretical account there is reason to believe conditions in the majority of these families would not have prepared the young to deal with questions of diversity and uncertainty in the work world, since they had been sheltered in intense, private homes until they were men; on another account, these homes provided exactly the kind of upbringing that would have adapted the young to the working conditions of shifting responsibilities and fragmentation involved in an economy becoming diverse in new and unforeseen ways. The variety of enterprise in Chicago during 1880, bespeaking a variety of conditions of life and labor later to make this city seem so unique, thus posed a specific problem about how the family had to adapt to urban life outside the home.

The working population of Union Park was distinctive apart from its occupational affluence in 1880. For the occupational structure formed part of a larger design of middle class working conditions for the people of Union Park; this larger design was composed of a series of prohibitions on certain groups from working, and a sorting of those who did work in terms of age and ethnic background.

PROHIBITIONS ON LABOR. The first prohibition on labor in Union Park concerned children. Virtually no children under ten worked; 92.2 percent of the children from ten to fourteen were not employed; in the ages from fifteen to nineteen, suddenly 54.4 percent were employed. It was in the middle to late teens that young people began to work in this community; the trials of child labor were largely unknown.

The second work prohibition was on the employment of illiterates. Although some adult men and women of all ages in the community were illiterate, they were not in the labor force at this time. Almost every laborer in Union Park was listed in the Census of 1880 as able to read and write (99.5 percent); 0.4 percent, or twenty-four workers, could neither read nor write, and five workers could not write. Surprisingly, of the handful who were illiterate, the native-born were a larger fragment than the foreign-born.

This literacy rate is astonishing — so much so that one begins to doubt the census takers counted anyone to whom they could not talk or who could not read the forms, a problem akin to the three million Americans "missing" in the 1960 Census.[10] Even granting some distortion, this literacy rate tells us also that very few Union Park people were crippled in their work in Chicago by virtue of not speaking the language (measures of literacy were in the English language). Of course, many of the foreigners in the community — Canadians, Englishmen, and Irish —

were from English-language groups; the Germans were the only sizable foreign-language group, and, it appears, most of them were bilingual.

The third set of sanctions in work that existed in Union Park during this year applied to women in the labor force. Women, especially unmarried women, could find work, yet the channels of labor open to them were quite narrow, and the pay they received was considerably less than that of men who labored at the same jobs.

In Union Park three fourths of all males worked, while only a quarter of the women did. On the other hand, this proportion was higher than that of the nation as a whole in 1880, where there were seven male workers to every female worker.[11] The explanation for this lies in a peculiar urban condition. The cities of the late nineteenth century tended to attract large numbers of single women, who migrated to large towns looking for better marriage prospects and a richer communal life than those found on the farm; these young women worked to sustain themselves until they married.[12] Such young unmarried women were the majority of the famale labor force in Union Park.

Women in Union Park who worked were concentrated in four major occupations: the majority were servants, fewer were clerks in stores, fewer still clerks in offices, and a handful were in professions, mostly teaching. The women workers in most of the four major occupations were predominantly unmarried: 95 percent of the women servants, 49 percent of the women clerks in stores, 81 percent of the women clerks in offices, 74 percent of the women professionals. In each of these areas save the last, advancing age and marriage led to withdrawal from work. For example, in 1880, women servants aged 20–25 constituted 30 percent of all women in this class; women aged 35–40 constituted only 6 percent of the servant total. Only women who taught remained a steady, and small, working group with advancing age.

The most marked characteristic of this female labor force was also the most discriminatory. As shown earlier in Table 6, for white collar workers, for industrial operatives, and for pieceworkers, women consistently made about half the salary of men in the same job categories. We do not know, of course, whether women were relegated to the lesser jobs in each of these broad divisions, and so made less money. But the effect on their pocketbooks remained the same in any case.

Two other features of work during the year 1880 gave Union Park its distinctive character. These acted not as prohibitions against work, but as mechanisms that sorted the population of workers into defined groups.

THE SOCIAL SORTING OF OCCUPATIONS. In the era of Andrew Carnegie and Horatio Alger, one popular myth by which the populace sustained itself was the gospel of unlimited opportunity: anyone, no matter what his age, birth, or religion, could succeed if only he tried hard enough. It was believed that there was nothing in the structure of society that would or could stand in the way of individual resolve and initiative. What was significant about this belief was its tenacity among Americans at the same time they experienced, as in Union Park, division in work, allied with forces like age or ethnic background, that had nothing to do with individual resolve.

Table 9 shows how the pattern of employment changed between young adulthood and middle age. Whether or not the change was due to a pattern of upward social mobility, in Union Park clearly there were some forms of labor tied to the age of the worker. This phenomenon seems to modern eyes a simple enough affair; advancement comes

Table 9. Age of persons in selected occupations[a]

Occupation	Ages 20–24	Ages 30–34	Ages 40–44	Ages 50–54
Executive	1.81%	3.57%	7.42%	7.94%
Proprietor	3.79	10.11	13.65	19.13
Clerk in office	26.48	19.88	16.46	14.07
Skilled laborer	8.37	10.71	7.83	10.83
Servant	27.50	9.64	8.43	2.16

[a] Columns do not total 100 percent because these are selected occupational groups.

usually through years of application. But a century ago, pictures of success like the Horatio Alger stories were of instant movement; the cultural pictures made the element of time at work less important than the act of will. In Union Park, there was absent what anthropologists call a "resonance" between cultural explanation and social fact, a split between what people of the time wanted to believe about the "openness" of the job system and the filtering they actually experienced. Further, this age sorting suggests how "appropriate" people might have felt their work to be: a middle-aged servant may have felt out of place and lost when so few of her generation were servants; a young girl of twenty-four may not have felt the invidious comparison since many young girls were servants. Similarly, a young executive, successful as he might have been, could also have felt out of place among his peers for being so unusual.

The second sorting of occupations occurred in the differences between native and foreign-born workers. As Table 10 shows, the white collar population was weighted toward native-born workers, while the blue collar population was more weighted to the foreign-born (with the exception of proprietary pursuits); in the blue collar ranks

Table 10. Nativity of adult workers in each occupational group[a]

White collar workers	Executive	Professionals	Arts	Proprietors	Clerks in office	Clerks in stores
American	78.7%	83.5%	71.2%	62.8%	75.2%	66.9%
Foreign	21.3	16.5	28.8	37.2	24.8	33.1
Total	100	100	100	100	100	100
	N = 254	N = 321	N = 146	N = 526	N = 1042	N = 857

Blue collar workers	Highly skilled laborers	Skilled laborers	Semiskilled laborers	Transport and communication	Unskilled laborers	Servants
American	75.8%	59.4%	63.3%	74.1%	63.5%	40.9%
Foreign	24.2	40.6	36.7	25.9	36.5	59.1
Total	100	100	100	100	100	100
	N = 149	N = 510	N = 286	N = 247	N = 178	N = 621

[a] Total number of workers in sample was 5129, of which 66.3% were American-born, 33.7% foreign-born.

the native-born were more dominant at the highest level. Accordingly, the income levels of the foreign-born workers as a whole were less than those of the native-born.

This pattern of occupations is striking, given the residential integration and similar family patterns of native and foreigner in Union Park. Nor were these foreigners Eastern or Southern European peasants; all the groups that were to inundate the American city by the opening of our own century were in 1880 absent. Why then, in this era before the great peasant migration to the cities, should these foreigners be less favored when they did not themselves possess that strangeness that later stereotyped the immigrant?

There are two contradictory explanations for this phenomenon. American society could have been so rigid in its sense of who belonged and who was an outsider that the sheer fact of being from abroad limited job opportunities. Some sorting, as discrimination, would have occurred in the city labor force, even though a sorting by family structure and residence did not occur in the community. Or, to take a less rigid view, there was something about the process of immigration itself that was disorienting for the migrants in dealing with the city. On this second interpretation, the trials the minority group experienced were not simply the discrimination a hostile majority brought to bear on them, but a process of dislocation that operated within the migrant or psychologically, as well as socially or from the outside. Anthropologists have long been familiar with the syndrome where primitive tribesmen who migrate to an urban area feel like they are not worthy in the new environment of anything but routine manual labor; the European farmers who migrated to the United States at the beginning of giant city growth might also have been susceptible to such "culture shock."

This line of reasoning suggests a broader approach for understanding Union Park's family life. For speculation of this kind makes more sense when it is put in the context of what anthropologists have called the culture shock of urban migration.

City "Culture Shock"

Chicago, we have seen, was a city that at this point in time possessed an unusually diversified occupational structure, one in which the workers of Union Park were spread throughout the white collar and upper blue collar echelons. The increasing of diversity in the economic world of the city posed a challenge to the families of Union Park: how would they prepare their young to cope with this diversity? On one account, that of Phillippe Ariès, the intense family life of Union Park should not have succeeded in this task; on another account, that of Talcott Parsons, it should have. The increase of economic and occupational diversity may may have produced a feeling of disorganization much like the culture shock of immigration, for the economy was producing a new set of diversities bewildering in their variety, uncertain to people of the time in their duration or viability. This confusion, this myriad of new and strange things a man might work at, could have posed the possibility for a feeling of being lost in work similar in its character to the feeling of being lost as a result of immigration. The question about the families of Union Park becomes not simply how "functional" they were in a mechanical sort of way but what kind of mechanisms of defense did they encourage in the young, against the shock of ever increasing diversity in work? It was not simply that there was a world beyond the family to be conquered, and that the fantasies of the time demanded men to act as conquerers; rather, this new city economy in Chicago contained the possibility for a continual series of dislocations, producing a feeling of unending instability, arising from the vigor of the economy itself.

This idea obviously adds a new element in weighing how family structure fitted people to be strong in their dealings with the larger society. This idea would "urbanize" the debate between Ariès and Parsons. The chain of reasoning gathers force when the structures of family described in the foregoing pages are seen as an ongoing process. For in this family process were concrete signs of a fearful "culture-shocked" life in the city.

6

THE STAGES OF FAMILY LIFE

In Union Park, a young father with three children faced problems unlike those of an older man with three adolescents about to strike out for themselves; the intimacy of a small nuclear home had, similarly, a different character for young people just starting out in the world than for old people who had lived together for many years. It is necessary to discover the character of family life for people at various stages of growth, in other words, in order to understand more fully the nature of the family bond itself. In Union Park, these stages presented a deeper and more complex picture of the ideas of "privacy" and "intimacy" by which writers like Parsons or Ariès have sought to typify the dominant, nuclear family structure. In the relations between family members of different ages were to be seen patterns of union and intensity amounting almost to a tyranny of these sedate and private homes over the people they sheltered.

The stages of the family cycle have been described in literature on the family in two ways. One is through a model devised by Kingsley Davis and Lloyd Warner, and amended by Talcott Parsons, which traces the changing lines of influence on or from an individual; this model tries to answer such questions as how an individual's obligations and sense of relatedness to his kin change as he grows older. The other major concept of the stages of family life has been formulated by the American psychoanalyst Erik Erikson, who brought to fruition certain rough ideas in the early writings of Freud. Erikson has sought to understand the life stages as periods dominated by different crises of growth in the psychic and social life of the individual, crises at first centered wholly in the arena of the family, but later broadening out to focus as well on the individual's relation to the larger society.[1] Both of these approaches, that of the changing lines of authority and that of the changing stress to which an individual feels himself subject, can be used to clarify the conditions of the life cycle for Union Park's families.

The materials from the Census of 1880 framed these family processes in a particular way, for the census data portrayed a complete picture of all age groups, but for one year only. Therefore in studying these age groups it is possible to look at concurrent family stages existing in the community during this year,[2] and thus form a truly "cross-sectional" portrait of family life.

Enrolling and Leaving School

Union Park parents enrolled their children in school in 1880 when the children were six or seven years old. The Census showed few children in school before five, nursery schools being rare at this time; most children, however, were in school by the age of ten; about 85 percent of the children between the ages of ten and fourteen were students.

It was in the sixteenth and seventeenth year that adolescents in the community rapidly dropped out. Whereas 75 percent of the fifteen-year-olds were in school, 60 percent of those sixteen, 32 percent of those seventeen, and 28 percent of those eighteen were in school. By age nineteen only a tenth remained in class. Thus the normal period of schooling was about eleven years from the age of six to the age of sixteen or seventeen. In 1880, the percentage of those who obtained high school diplomas when they left school was very low, about 2.5 percent.[3] However, those youngsters who left school before graduation day were not what we would now call dropouts, because men and women of that time did not need high school degrees as a certificate of fitness for work, as they do now.

Yet there was a significant group of children who were dropouts within the school situation of a century ago. About 8.1 percent of the children in Union Park between the ages of ten and fourteen were neither working nor studying, and the incidence of temporary or permanent disabilities during the year cannot account for their numbers. We know nothing of these children other than the fact they existed; perhaps they suffered emotional or mental problems the family would not admit, or perhaps they were kept home, as child laborers around the house.

The older adolescents leaving school shared much in common: neither the ethnicity of their fathers, nor the type of kinship structure in which they lived, seemed to influence when the children would leave, nor did the occupational class of their fathers. The rhythms of attending and leaving school were evidently a feature of life in this middle class community that cut across the lines of birth, kinship, and parental status.

The pattern of what an adolescent boy did on leaving school was clear: he went to work. In Union Park the strength of this flow from school to work is striking; there were few young men who held off from working in this year, who took what Erikson has called a "moratorium" from engagement in the activity which would occupy most of their adult lives, gainful labor. Of the total group of male adolescents aged fifteen to nineteen, only 7 percent were neither in school nor at work during the year; for the age group of young men from 20 to 24 the figure was lower.

A different pattern seemed to prevail in the middle class families of European cities. In Germany, the "Wanderjahre," the years of a young man's wandering and touring, had roots in the culture of the Romantic Age and were a routine feature of life for prosperous families until the opening of the present century; in Paris, a middle class youth often expected his parents to provide for a year or two of freedom before entering a career. In Chicago itself, the percentage of youths who neither worked nor attended schools in 1880 was higher than that to be found in Union Park, although this community was itself a youthful one, having many more young people in its midst, proportionately, than the rest of the city. These comparisons suggest that in Union Park there was strong pressure to get into one's life work as soon as schooling was finished, a pressure stronger than that middle class adolescents elsewhere experienced.[4]

The adolescent girls of Union Park were more favored in this respect. Sizable numbers of girls did find a period of moratorium for themselves: two thirds of the fifteen- to nineteen-year-old girls who did not work in 1880 also did not attend school; of this group seven out of eight were unmarried. Evidently, the community allotted a period of retreat to the women, with only assistance around the home as a duty, that it did not accord to the men; these young women had a chance to forego the school discipline of childhood without immediately adopting the adult role of wife or woman at work.

Leaving Home

In the families of Union Park, the breaking away of young people from the home of their parents occurred in an unorganized, formless way; there were no points of demarcation, like graduation from high school or college, where suddenly large groups of young people found themselves on their own. But in almost all families, by the time the sons left home they had also married, so that there were few instances of two generations of conjugal families living in the same household. The pattern, then, was clearly one of the young breaking away to found families of their own.

A family break in Union Park, so uncertain in timing while so final, might thus have been more emotionally weighted than in middle class families of today, when we expect the children to leave at certain "appropriate" times. The economics of the family of course added to this strain of separation. When a working son left the fold, so did his contribution to the rent, the food, and the other household expenses. The unpredictability of this loss in Union Park families must have made family plans difficult to pursue, and perhaps made the break seem like unfair desertion.

This process is first revealed by the ages at which young men broke away from their parental home. In the age group from fifteen to nineteen, 90.5 percent of the young men were under the protection of a family head, with 9.5 percent living alone, in single-member families. For young adult men from twenty to thirty years old the question was not whether they were breaking from their parents' home, but the rate at which they did so. By the end of their twenties, a majority of these young people were still unmarried and living at home; in the twenty to twenty-four age group, 71.9 percent were under the protection of someone else, and in the twenty-five to twenty-nine age group, 55.4 percent were. In the age group of the thirties this situation was reversed; two thirds of those men in their early thirties and four fifths of those in their late thirties were heads of households.

The fact that a majority of those in their twenties were dependent on another household head, and a majority of those in their thirties were not, is a statistical convention of significance: a "majority" is not per se a turning point. Socially, rather, the data represent a long slide into household responsibility from the outset of adulthood into the late thirties.[5] Thus there was no sudden cutting loose from the family at the outset of legal adulthood; rather, the process of breaking away, which there is good reason to believe was a painful one, was much more protracted.

The women of Union Park left their parents' home much earlier than the men: what took men, as a group, fifteen to twenty years to accomplish took the women five to ten. Three out of five women were married or living alone by the time they were thirty, and of those in their thirties, almost all lived elsewhere than with their parents.

While the women earned an earlier independence from their parents than the men, few of them expressed it in living alone in Union Park; only 5.4 percent of women between the ages of twenty and twenty-four and only 7.7 percent of those twenty-five to thirty did so. Instead, most of the women who left their parents' home, did so to marry. Given the weakness and innocence of the world women were supposed to embody by the standards of the day, the small number of independent young women may not be surprising; what is surprising is that the men, once having broken from their parents, exercised the option of living alone little more than did girls. This absence of great numbers of lone women, or men, grew out of the special conditions by which marriage took place in Union Park.

Founding a Family

It has been shown that the young men leaving school took no moratorium before entering their adult role as worker. In the same way, young people in Union Park did not leave a gap between shelter in their parents' home and the founding of their own homes.

Of the few men age twenty to twenty-four who had broken away from home, about a third were married. In the late twenties and early thirties, about three fourths of those who had broken away from home were married, and almost all of those aged thirty-five to thirty-nine heading a household were married. The social picture this indicates is that after twenty-five, the point of breaking from a parent's home was for the purpose of getting married.

This conclusion, seemingly so innocuous, in fact tells a great deal about the sources of stability in the Union Park families. A young man stayed within the orbit of his family until he was ready to found the same orbit with himself in a different position — rather like playing the same game with the players changed. The unfolding of the stages of life seem to have been rooted to the same family structures: marriage in predominantly small, nuclear homes. The process of change was a process of changing roles in this structure.

Here, surely, was a sign of the power of the family in the lives of the Union Park people. The break of sons from the homes of their fathers was not a "generation gap" as the current phrase has it, did not pit stable fathers against errant sons. A young man in this city did not cast off the ways of his parents; he worked rather than wandered, and in his late twenties or early thirties, when he was ready to cease being under the dominion of his parents, he did not give himself up to the freedom of being alone but instead became a husband, and in this way took the place of his father.

It used to be fashionable to ascribe to the great city the capacity to break apart the home, and lead even respectable young men astray in pursuit of an unbridled freedom. But in Union Park, these young urbanites from good homes followed, if anything, an opposite course. In the midst of the great diversity of population and styles of life taking form in Chicago at this time, the young people of Union Park clung to relations of dependence and responsibility they knew as children, only now the young sons were responsible for others, rather than to them. The unmanageable and overwhelming forces of the city as a whole might have had a hand in this continuity across the generations. The sheltering homes of Union Park could have served as a refuge for the sons, when they came to maturity in the midst of a confusing urban order.

Marriages in Union Park were not then simply a transition to adulthood, they occurred within adulthood. By contrast, in 1957, the median age of first marriage in the United States was twenty-one years of age; for this Chicago community in 1880, only 20.4 percent of the young adults twenty to twenty-four had married.[6] The composite picture for men and women in Union Park in 1880 is as follows.

Age group	Percentage married
15–19	3.5
20–24	20.4
25–29	43.0
30–34	60.3
35–39	70.7
40–44	72.0

Marriage occurred, then, after most of the men and many of the women had been at work for some years. Again, there is a contrast to the modern situation, wherein most of the middle class population does not begin to work until after a college education, that is, until the time which is also the median age of marriage. The people of Union Park, especially the men, were launched in the work world well before they considered founding a home.

The people of this community who married were also more widely separated in age than the married couples of modern times. In the period following World War II, the median difference in ages between spouses has never been more than 3.5 years, and the closer one comes to the present day, the more men and women marrying for the first time tend to be of equal age, about twenty-one years old.[7]

In Union Park, only a third of the married couples had ages within five years of each other. Furthermore, the lower the age of the wife, the less likely would be marriage with a man in the same age group. Whereas 27 percent of the women 26 to 30 had husbands aged 26 to 30, only 17.9 percent of the women 21 to 25 had husbands aged 21 to 25, and only 7.1 percent of the wives aged 16 to 20 had husbands aged 16 to 20.

In the majority of cases, the husband was at least five to ten years older than the wife; for about a fifth of the married couples, the husband was ten to fifteen years older than the wife; and in the case of wives under twenty-five, from 10 to 15 percent of their spouses were fifteen to twenty years older than they themselves.

Why did this age gap exist? Some psychologists treat differences in age between modern couples as a sign that men want to marry women whose experience of the world is unequal to their own. The explanation cannot be so simple historically. There exists scant statistical material on the age of marriage earlier in the nineteenth century,[8] but to judge from novels — one thinks, for example, of the liaisons in Jane Austen's domestic novels — marriages between girls newly out of their teens and men in their middle or late thirties were taken to be between partners who treated each other as equals. Historically it makes more sense to look at these age differences in terms of family economics.

It is plausible that these age differences existed in Union Park because the women felt they ought to marry men who were "established," that a marriage in which both partners worked to create occupational or financial security was not as "good." Such an explanation would mean the man was expected to bring a kind of dowry to the bride, in the form of assurance of his financial worth, a reversal of the older village pattern. In other words, he must seem a good match, materially, to her, rather than she, and her dowry, a point of appeal to him.

In *The Elegant Eighties,* Herma Clark described the strains of such a situation in one middle class Chicago household of the 1880's. A young girl was affianced to a doctor in his late twenties, but they were waiting to marry until he had firmly established himself in his career; the wait was long, however, and at one point the young girl threatened to desert the young man for someone older who could marry her right away. In good Victorian fashion, virtue triumphed in the end: the older man was revealed as a lecherous blackguard, and the girl returned to the steadfast doctor. It is easily imaginable, however, that in many cases the strain of waiting might have been too much, so that women would turn to older men who were ready to found a family.

It would be difficult to prove statistically the frequency of this psychological-economic situation. Many more men married in their thirties than their twenties in Union Park, and the reasonable explanation for this would be because they were more able to support a family. In turn, it seems plausible that men would have to wait for conjugal bliss until they were economically stable — something the married couples of our own time do not wait for — because they and their future spouses believed it necessary for the man to have "proved," economically, that he was capable of being a husband.[9]

Thus a man's power in the work world became a precondition of his marital virtue. His success as a worker in young adulthood counted for much more than immediate material gain; it also helped form his attractiveness as a male and future mate.

If such an explanation does violence to present notions of romantic love, if the rational and calculative element seems to have played too great a hand here, it should be pointed out that the residents of Union Park enjoyed an extremely low rate of overt divorce; only 44 out of 8000 adults were listed as divorced. The men and women of Union Park may not have given themselves to each other wholly out of romantic love, but they wanted to pledge themselves for good. The strength, the sanctification almost, of the marital bond was revealed by the kind of sacrifices young people made for it.[10]

Apart from material considerations, how did people in Union Park go about choosing a partner in marriage?

Most of the *parents* of the adults in Union Park in 1880 did not cross cultural lines in choosing their mates. There were few instances in which native-born mothers chose foreign-born husbands — 2.3 percent — and fewer instances where a native-born father chose a foreign wife — 1.7 percent; Americans had married Americans, and foreigners taken "their own kind."

The adults of Union Park as of 1880 began to break this barrier, for they showed more of a tendency to intermarry across native-foreign lines than did their parents. The figures available concerned married couples with children, and are presented in Table 11. Compared to a total inter-

Table 11. Rate of intermarriage, by age of children

	Age of children				
	0 to 2	3 to 4	5 to 9	10 to 14	15 to 19
Both parents native	50%	49%	52%	49%	44%
Father native	7	7	6	6	4
Mother native	13	10	10	9	5
Both parents foreign	31	36	33	35	47
Total	100[a]	100	100	100	100
	N = 528	N = 352	N = 846	N = 761	N = 1079

[a] Rounded off.

marriage rate of 8.9 percent among the parents of the adults in Union Park, there was a 19.3 percent rate of intermarriage among the adults in Union Park with small infants. These adults were, as would be expected, among the youngest of the married couples in Union Park.

Why had these young adults started to break, in part, a pattern of marriage choice so rigid in their own parents' generation? The impulse behind the migration of young people to American cities at this time provides a partial explanation. Writers like Arthur Schlesinger, Sr., have characterized the urban migration after the Civil War as in part a voluntary movement of young people in search of a more exciting, richer life than that available on the farms. In Union Park it appears that some young people were experimenting with more complex forms of social life through crossing cultural boundaries in choosing mates. These young people were creating a certain richness in the fabric of the community by marrying foreigners; especially was this true of the young American women in Union Park, who had a higher intermarriage rate than young American men.

Having said this, there must be added a somewhat somber note on ethnicity and marriage age. The census data show that more of the foreign-born population remained single into middle age than was true for native Americans. This would accord with the conclusion that marriage took place at the point where economic stability and self-sufficiency could be demonstrated to a marriage partner. Foreign-born males were not as established in the better, white collar jobs as native-born workers, and so would have had longer to wait in order to be "ready" for marriage. This conclusion, while logically plausible, is, humanly, somewhat discouraging; a sizable body of men had to wait until they were into their forties to enjoy a domestic life and have children.

Adding Children to the Family: The Tensions of Birth Control

In the previous chapter, the size of families in the middle class homes of Union Park was shown to be relatively small, compared to the post–Civil War, dominantly rural, family pattern. While in Union Park the form of kinship and the ethnic background of the parents had some influence on family size, the boundaries were steady at a maximum of six related kin to a household; the average size was 3.9 people to a family, and most nuclear families had only one or two children.

At the end of the nineteenth century, the great urbanist Adna Ferrin Weber sought to explain urban, middle class family size like that found in Union Park as follows: "a declining birthrate accompanies an advancing civilization. Insofar as cities represent the highest culture and comfort of a country, just so far will they have a low birth rate and families below the average size." [11] Given an expanding birthrate in the large cities of the modern era, such a general explanation no longer seems convincing. Rather, the forces shaping family size in a community like Union Park are to be found in that culture's attitude toward the sexual relations proper to married men and women.

In a pioneering study of these family relations, Oscar Handlin has shown that while some means of artificial control were known, their use was stigmatized by all organized professional groups of the society: "The Church, the state, and the medical profession united in condemning every artificial practice to limit the size of families. Birth control, like abortion, it was said, enfeebled the frame and produced a horrible train of disease. It was also a crime against nature and God, as well as against the state." [12] This meant that sexual relations in marriage could assume only one purpose: the procreation of children. Yet intercourse between a man and his wife was to be consummated ideally once every three years, since this was considered the proper spacing between children.[13] If this seems unreal, we should recall that the prohibition worked in Union Park. It worked because the taboo was in turn part of a larger web of sexual repression. A man who was respectable was supposed to feel sexually aroused no more than once a month, in cycle with the lunar change,[14] and, as described in the researches of both Steven Marcus and Handlin, normal adolescent practices like masturbation were thought to lead to the most terrible physical and moral horrors. Further, the period of pregnancy was subject to intense anxiety: "During pregnancy and lactation total abstinence was requisite; indeed, then the considerate husband would not even share his wife's room lest he use 'up one half or more of the natural supply of oxygen, which God, in His Providence, had designed for her.' " [15]

This moral and emotional climate was made more rigid by the economics of family size, at least in city communities resembling Union Park. The addition of children was a liability on the family's resources for at least fifteen years, since youngsters did not work but went to school, and, unlike the farm family, could not naturally participate at all ages in the household economy. Handlin singles out this economic disadvantage of children to be most pressing for urban middle class groups similar to those in Union Park, for these parents had to make positive economic contributions to their children's welfare, as well as receiving nothing from them economically. "It was a drain on family resources to give children a proper start in life . . . Most difficult of all was the situation of the middle groups in cities; their children required education and capital if they were to avoid a disastrous fall in status. Everywhere was a half-expressed desire to limit the number of births." [16]

If one sought to locate in Union Park the group of young people most deeply in conflict, most anxious about their family situation, surely it would not be the rebellious wandering youth of the community — there being, in any event, few of these wanderers — but young adults just married. The men, predominantly, had waited out their twenties to be able to afford to leave home and marry; yet the moment legal and moral sanction was accorded them to express themselves in their bodies, an even more rigid set of taboos denied them that expression. Again, as before marriage, their lives became a waiting game, governed by their willpower, between ineradicable physical urges and the economic and moral codes by which they lived.

Some of this tension must in its turn have affected the way these young couples treated their children. Fear, resentment, shame — these are the emotions one can imagine young parents feeling toward their infants at this time, emotions that may have poisoned something of the love of parents for their newborn.

The social means by which family size was controlled, then, shows how the strains of sexuality were here historical, not simple "innate" psychologically or biologically. For given the moral taboos, the marriage process, and the economics of society in Union Park, early marriage must have been marked by great tension; all forces of this community worked toward the centrality of the home in the lives of its people, yet the sexual bond of marriage acquired an abstractness and distance through these taboos that denied the physical experience of intimacy between man and wife.

There also existed in Union Park defined ways the family tie could be broken: through a failure in marriage, through failure to marry, or through the inevitable deaths in old age that left widows and widowers.

Breaks in the Family

The breaking of a family through divorce or desertion was an area of greater moral sensitivity a century ago than in our own time. What we have come to regard as personal tragedy was once taken as ethical failure; a family had a responsibility to stay together, apart from the personal inclination of the marriage partners. If that responsibility were not met, the family was disgraced. Thus it is difficult now to feel the shock of a play like Ibsen's *A Doll's House* as his audience must have felt it, difficult now to see why Dreiser's *Sister Carrie* evoked cries of outrage from his public, when it seems so clear that Dreiser condemned his heroine. Divorce was to that earlier era an act in which the family idea, as the symbol of cultural order, stood violated.

It is thus not surprising that divorce was a rare phenomenon in Union Park, 44 out of 8056 adults being divorced (with no reported instances of desertion). But forces of breakup were at work concealed behind these official figures. In a general study, Talcott Parsons has found evidence that the rate of hidden marital separation at the end of the nineteenth century may have been greater than it is today.[17] Brody's work on the Polish steelworkers has shown that it was common for a young immigrant to come to this country alone and send for his family when he had enough funds to support them. It seems reasonable that some American-born, rural migrants to this Chicago community might have done the same thing, so that they would temporarily have broken off from their families on the farms. Both suppositions, that of concealed desertions and that of temporary family disintegration in the process of urban migration, might explain conjugal breaks revealed by the data, but not encompassed in the Census' simple tabulation of divorce.

Among the 855 people who lived totally alone in the community, without any other kin members, 99 were married men and 14 were married women. Among nuclear families or extended families with at least two kin members present, 184 were families with the wife absent, and 34 were families with the husband absent; these form part of a group of 2,139 families in which both husbands and wives should have been present. Families with absent wife or husband thus accounted for 10.9 percent of this group.

If the number of married, singe-member families be added to the number of absent-wife or absent-husband families with other kin present, there were 331 conjugally broken families in all, about a tenth of the total number of families. Lynn Lees found in London at this time, by contrast, only half as many broken families in a comparable middle class area, and only a third as many broken families in a poor Irish section.[18]

There is little to be learned about the broken families in Union Park from the Census of 1880 save the ages of married individuals living alone. Such people were not young adults primarily; their ages spread throughout middle age. The image of young husbands come to the city in order to earn money to bring the rest of the family thus does not fit. There may have been middle-aged husbands engaged in this kind of migration, but a man who pulled up stakes in the middle of his working and familial life would be undertaking an enterprise more disruptive and more dangerous than if he were just starting a job or family.

The existence of so much hidden separation or desertion in Union Park, both in itself or in comparison to the situation in the London communities Lees studies, is a striking phenomenon. For if any community in Chicago should have been stable in its family coherence, surely it was this respectable, staid, and dull residential area. Whether in a working-class section of Chicago the rate would have been lower, as in London, is not now known. These one-in-ten marriages of Union Park that were broken indicate, in any event, a dimension of disorganization during the initial stages of middle class urban life.

This family disorganization may help explain why the men of the time put such a premium on the family itself, accorded it such sanctity that events like official divorce were taken as moral failure. For if the conjugal unit was imperiled during the growth of the industrial city among upright and respectable people, the attempt to preserve its stability through enshrining the family, making it a font of goodness, would follow naturally. Whether this process is described in elaborate terms of "cognitive dissonance theory" or simply as defensiveness, the act of protecting a value or institution becoming unstable by making it a moral virtue is a common pattern; if this Union Park family instability were widespread in the rest of American middle class society, one source of the value placed on the family at the time comes clear.

The power of the family as an institution in Union Park was reflected in the rapid decrease in the number of bachelors and spinsters in the middle-aged population. Among people in their late thirties, 21.5 percent were unmarried; 17.1 percent of those aged forty to forty-four were unmarried, 9.9 percent of those aged forty-five to forty-nine were unmarried. Few bachelors or spinsters of middle age remained under the parental roof; the pattern was for them to live either by themselves or with married brothers or sisters.

It has already been shown how proportionately more of the foreign-born than native-born population lived in middle age as bachelors or spinsters; there were sex differences in the total pattern of nonmarriage as well, for up to the age of fifty, a higher proportion of the men remained unmarried; after this point, there were an equal number of bachelors and spinsters in Union Park.

Women in Union Park, as today, possessed a longer life

span than men, and thus were much more frequently left alone in old age when their mates died; the data on the community are shown in Table 12. Because women characteristically did not work during their adult years, the na-

Table 12. Widows and widowers, by age

	40–44	45–49	50–54	55–59	60–64	65–99
Percentage who are widowers	6%	5%	8%	9%	12%	28%
Percentage who are widows	14	24	26	33	53	70
Total	20[a]	29	34	41	65	98
	100% N = 789	N = 563	N = 470	N = 295	N = 207	N = 238

[a] Equals less than 100 percent because rest of age group is married or single.

ture of their loss was compounded; both emotional and material support was taken from them in their later years.

Breaks in the family due to the death of a spouse were associated with kinship differences, by and large, in that widows went to live with their married children, and so created some extended families. Thus, at the end of a lifetime, a shift in family form from that experienced by most adult age groups occurred; with advancing age, the nuclear forms ceased to shelter those elderly who had lost a mate, and who now had to make an adaptation to forms of family most of them had previously not experienced. Whether this shift in family scene was a painful event or not, the numbers will never tell us; yet it does seem reasonable to suppose that those left did experience a powerful jolt, in that the shock of a family death was again compounded by the need to live in a new kind of family.

Overview: The Meaning of Intensity
in the Forming of the Family

The stages of family life portrayed in the Census of 1880 revealed in Union Park patterns of marked intensity and strength in the family bond. The young did not leave the parental home, for the most part, until they themselves were ready to marry. For young men this meant that a majority were living under the parental roof until the third decade of their lives; it was possible for the young women to leave the home of their parents at an earlier point, but only to marry. Few of the young men were alone in 1880, or living as wanderers without occupation; the end of the discipline of school marked the beginning of the discipline of work. Indeed, the patterns of age and marriage in Union Park strongly suggest that the young men waited to move to homes of their own until they had established themselves in work, so that success in the economic order of the city came to be joined to the "adequacy" of a young man for marriage. The offspring of these marriages were limited, as the statistics on the community evidence. Modern research suggests strong cultural pressures against artificial means of birth control and toward abstinence as the single regulator of the family's size. A host of sexual taboos and the prohibition of child labor in this middle class community made abstinence not only possible but a compelling necessity. The economic influence on the family bond, and the continual presence of the small, nucleated family in the lives of young people moving from childhood to marriages of their own, were alloyed to some extent by the greater experimentation among the young of this community in forming marriages across ethnic lines.

All of these phenomena gave a concrete meaning to the

intense family as Parsons and Ariès describe it. A guiding force was fear: fear of marrying too soon or having too many children, fear of not being stable. Indeed, the undercurrents of desertion and separation in Union Park would have led to the same end; the family was enshrined out of a sense of its peril in the city. The power of the family portrayed in these life stages, combined with its isolated position as the sole primary group, are the terms by which these urban families were inward-turning worlds of their own.

7

THE TIES OF FAMILY AND WORK

In Union Park, the struggle for economic survival did not take place in the home, as was the case in the home workshops of pre-industrial cities. It did not even take place within the borders of Union Park, since there were few shops and no factories from the post-fire boom left in the community by 1880. Most of the people from these solid respectable families commuted far downtown to work in the large stores and the office skyscrapers beginning to rise in the new, giant city. And yet, between the great offices and the small, sheltered homes around Union and Jefferson Parks, lines of marked influence and interaction were drawn in this year; the cast of family life, the character of it, was inseparable from the labors of fathers, sons, and more rarely, daughters downtown.

Such connections are, of course, comfortable to Marxist thinkers, who presume a direct line of influence from work to family form, so that the economic structure "causes" the family to assume certain shapes. Thus, in the fascinating work of Friedrich Engels on the family, the intense, inward-turning family is treated as a system of slavery created by the wage slavery of capitalism.[1] In a community study, it is necessary to be a little more timid, and explore the lines of association between home and office, as in this

Chicago neighborhood, without presuming in advance to understand their reasons for being. That there was a mutual influence between family and work in Union Park is not disputable.

Work and the Relations between Family Members

HOW WORK AFFECTED THE BALANCES OF AUTHORITY IN THE FAMILY. The presence of the work world was most immediately felt in the family circle when the lines of authority in the home were upset by special work experiences. This violation of normal authority patterns was intragenerational: relations between older brother and younger brother, or husband and wife, could be disrupted through an imbalance in occupational achievement.

What unity or disunity might brothers have felt toward each other in Union Park as a result of their work? Table 13 shows the patterns of occupation among older and

Table 13. Occupations of older and younger brothers

	Older brother	Younger brother
Executive and professional	11.6%	4.7%
Proprietor	9.3	9.3
Clerical	50.0	59.3
Skilled manual	22.1	19.8
Unskilled manual	7.0	7.0
Total	100	100
		N = 172 pairs of brothers

younger sons who were living with their fathers during the year 1880. On the surface little difference is apparent between younger and older sons. Slightly more of the older brothers engaged in upper-status white collar pursuits, and correspondingly more of the younger brothers engaged in clerical work. There is nothing startling in this, since the older brother had more time to work himself up. But hidden in these statistics is a human situation of some pain.

In families where the elder worked in some form of manual labor in 1880, his younger brother, in the majority of cases, held a white collar job. While among older brothers who were white collar workers, there was a 5 percent incidence of younger brothers holding jobs with higher status, among older brothers who were blue collar workers there was a 56 percent incidence of younger brothers holding white collar jobs.

Here, surely, was a potential for strain in the family, produced by occupational patterns. Normal sibling rivalries might not have been disturbed in homes where the elder son was a white collar worker, for his younger brother, presumably less knowledgeable in the ways of the world, seldom occupied a higher position than his own. In those families where the elder son was a manual laborer, his "little brother" was in a majority of cases established in white collar work that paid much more than his own labor. In such families, routine patterns of guidance and deference between brothers might well have been upset. Thus could the issue of work have become a source of tension in the attitudes of sons toward each other.

The group of working women who were married had a special pattern of job holding, one that could lead to a similar imbalance in authority relations in the family. The majority of these working wives were store clerks (53 percent), followed by those who were artists (15 percent), and those who were clerks in an office (11 percent); the profession of teaching as well as the menial work of a servant were occupations not carried into marriage. A second contrast between working wives and the female labor force as a whole was that the percentage of wives who worked (7 percent) was much lower than that of women in general (about 25 percent).

For those wives in Union Park who did work, what relations did their jobs bear to the labor done by their husbands? One might expect that the poorer the husband, the more likely would be his wife to work. Given that the people of the study were from a middle class community of the late nineteenth century, we would be tempted to affirm this even more strongly, for the respectable wife was supposed to remain within the home, and her having to work signified a loss in status for the whole family.

The census findings on the people of Union Park did not support this expectation. Of the working wives 33 percent had husbands engaged in high status white collar occupations, 30 percent had husbands in lower status white collar work, 18 percent had husbands in skilled manual labor, and 19 percent had husbands in semiskilled or unskilled or servant labor. This distribution of jobs among the husbands of working wives reflected the general pattern of job distribution in the community. Wives of poor men were not employed to a much greater degree than those whose husbands were more affluent. There was a striking reason why this was so.

In Union Park there was a greater identity of husband-wife jobs when the husband worked in the upper reaches of the occupation ladder than when he worked in the lower ranks. The wives of lower white collar and blue collar workers tended to hold better jobs than their husbands. It was especially common for the wives of industrial laborers to work as a clerk in an office, and clerical work of this type paid much more at this time than did industrial labor. Seldom was the wife of an industrial worker to be found laboring in a sweatshop or as a domestic.

This suggests that in Union Park a working wife presented a weaker challenge to her husband's status when the husband was himself a white collar worker than in homes where the man was a blue collar worker; in the latter case the work the wife performed, and consequently the amount of money she brought to the family, meant she had the material power to challenge her husband's position as leader of the home. Thus, while a wife's working might not have been innately disruptive to the psychological balance between husband and wife in a white collar family, the peculiar position of the working wife whose husband was a manual laborer may have offered a challenge to the authority patterns in the family.

This situation helps explain why the number of working wives in Union Park was so small in that spectrum of society where economic need would lead one to expect many wives to be at work. It cannot be known, statistically, if the possibility for friction between working wives and their blue collar husbands actually materialized, but how else is the great absence of working women in the laborer classes to be explained when wages for their husbands were so low, and the conditions of employment so uncertain? Married blue collar working men were distributed throughout the age scale, so that their wives cannot be assumed to have been specially burdened with young children; some other, inner restraint tied them to the home as strongly as their neighbors whose husbands could afford to have a nonworking wife. The familial imbalance between working husband and working wife in the laboring classes offers a clear explanation: increased income was sacrificed, on this account, for emotional stability and peace within the home, so that the man could remain regnant in his responsibility for the family.

Peculiar intragenerational strains thus existed among

both young and old in the working class families of Union Park. In the relations between husbands who were manual laborers and their wives, in the relations between elder sons who were manual laborers and their younger brothers, there existed patterns of labor that could challenge the supremacy of the father or of the older, more experienced brother in the family hierarchy. Among the white collar, middle class families who dominated Union Park, work posed a different kind of family problem. In these homes, intergenerational patterns of work between father and son were sources of strain in the transmission of authority in the home. For between fathers and sons stood a grave problem: would the sons be able to maintain, through their work, the middle class status of the family?

WORK AND THE PASSING ON OF AUTHORITY IN THE FAMILY. Work intruded into the family lives of those fathers, in their early and middle forties, who in 1880 had sons working in the city. It was the gap between what these fathers and sons did, when they left by carriage or horse trolley every morning to go to their offices or shops, that marked their relations, and provides a clue to the puzzle of the father's position in his home.

Table 14 shows what work was performed by sons twenty-one and over and their fathers in six major occupational groups. Most of these sons, as shown in Chapter Six, had been at work for more than four years. (The last of the occupational groups of parents, those retired or not working, was not dominantly composed of men. Of this group 39 percent were men who had retired, 61 percent were widows who were living with their working sons but not themselves at work. All the other occupational groups were composed almost exclusively of men.)

The figures in Table 14 indicate that in Union Park

Table 14. Occupations of household heads and their sons in 1880

	Occupation of head of household					
Occupation of son	Executives or professionals	Proprietors	Clerical workers	Skilled manual laborers	Unskilled laborers	Retired or not working
Executives or professionals	18%	8%	5%	14%	9%	17%
Proprietors	3	34	2	0	0	15
Clerical workers	50	50	70	41	27	43
Skilled manual laborers	18	8	20	39	9	21
Unskilled laborers	11	0	4	7	55	3
Total	100	100	100	100	100	100
	(N = 76)	(N = 76)	(N = 112)	(N = 88)	(N = 22)	(N = 134)

there did not exist a capacity for sons from good families uniformly to establish themselves in a better working position than sons from poor families. Young men from the homes of skilled laborers were almost as numerous in executive or professional work as boys from the homes of executives or professionals. Although clerical workers were better paid at the time than skilled laborers, sons from the families of clerical workers were not able to reach into these high status positions to the extent the sons from the working class families were. The same diversity existed in the white collar groups themselves: the sons of proprietors were able to establish themselves in great numbers as proprietors, a sharing of occupation that did not occur for fathers and sons in the executive or professional offices. Young men from the families of Union Park proprietors fell into manual labor to the extent of only 8 percent in this year, while 29 percent of the young men from executive families did manual labor.

In only one major occupation did a majority of the Union Park sons pursue the occupations of their fathers: about 70 percent of the sons of clerical workers were themselves clerical workers. (Little can be determined of the sons of unskilled labor, since their numbers were so small.) One occupation, proprietorship, seemed inaccessible to the sons from clerical and working class homes; evidently, at this early point in their careers, such sons did not possess the capital required to start or buy a small store of their own.

Why these patterns of dispersion up and down occurred in 1880 in Union Park will be explored in Part Three, by looking at family and labor over the course of two decades. The materials for this year alone suggest, though, a set of forces at work in Union Park different from those indicated for London by Seebohm Rowntree in his "cycle of poverty" concept. Rowntree envisioned monetary but not occupational gains made by the sons of the proletariat in the ages from twenty to thirty, and then, with increased family burdens, a decline in funds back into poverty; by contrast, the sons of manual laborers in Union Park made occupational moves to white collar positions at this beginning point in their own careers. For the sons from both poor and affluent homes in Union Park, the human question embedded in these patterns of dispersion was what effect they had on the fear or the expectations fathers had of their young in the world outside the home.

From the parental point of view, there must have been a sharp division within the most "respectable" classes in Union Park as to the capabilities and prospects of the sons of the well-to-do. The proprietors seemed to have cause for little worry; their sons, in this year, either followed in the parental footsteps or were engaged in clerical work. But in that occupational group whose status was determined by its high place in the industrial and administrative bureaucracies of the city, rather than in the concrete, property-based ownership of a business, there must have been more cause for alarm. The executives and professionals who had achieved good positions in what, at this point in the nineteenth century, were new kinds of economic enterprises — enterprises involving profits, personnel, and administrative complexity unknown in the earlier farms and small towns of America — found their sons dispersed into the ranks of men who worked with their hands as much as into the high-level positions to which they themselves belonged. And, as shown in Table 15, among those young people in their own midst, the next generation of executives and professionals, the backgrounds were almost as much working class as professional.

Such intergenerational dispersion in this new, explora-

Table 15. Parental background of sons at work in 1880

	Occupation of sons				
Occupation of father	Executives and professionals	Proprietors	Clerical workers	Skilled manual laborers	Unskilled laborers
Executives and professionals	23%	4%	15%	13%	24%
Proprietors	10	52	15	6	0
Clerical workers	10	4	31	21	12
Skilled manual laborers	19	0	14	32	18
Unskilled laborers	3	0	2	2	35
Retired or not working	36	40	23	26	12
Total	100	100	100	100	100
	(N = 62)	(N = 50)	(N = 254)	(N = 106)	(N = 34)

tive, urban branch of middle class life may help us account for a phenomenon of the late nineteenth century that historians have treated as a kind of psychological quirk, an irrational feeling: the intense fear of falling into poverty. The sudden collapse of a family's fortunes — a theme seen in all manner of literature of the time, from *Vanity Fair* and the "dime novels" to, at century's end, Lily Bart's father in *The House of Mirth* — involved the ruin caused by the sudden failure of the family head, usually in some disaster on the stock exchange. The Union Park data suggest that perhaps the place to look for the source of this fear of a sudden plunge into poverty, in nonfictional lives, is not the state of the head of the "respectable" household, but rather the position of his sons. It seems, from the statistical material, that the achievement of one generation was not, at this one point in time, duplicated in the next; from a psychological viewpoint, the heads of "respectable" households may have felt insecure out of fear not for themselves but for their offspring.

This idea cuts deeper. The data showed that half the sons of executives and professionals and half the sons of proprietors were engaged in clerical, white collar work. But, as Table 15 makes clear, these clerical jobs were also filled by large numbers of the sons of lower white collar and manual laborers. It would be reasonable, indeed predictable, if upper middle class fathers worried not a little that their sons were thrown amongst the sons of "lesser" men at the start of their careers, if, despite all the talk of "free enterprise" among these respectable men, they did not wish that their sons were given some special advantage. The workings of a polyglot job market could be frightening when lesser men have moved up, through vigor and ambition, in a position to compete with one's own son, who was perhaps shielded for most of his life from the hard realities of the competitive world.

If anxiety prevailed among executive fathers in respect to their sons' careers, at the other end of the social scale there certainly was cause for hope. The majority of the sons from working class homes had white collar jobs in 1880, including a sizeable fragment in junior executive positions. The lower middle class clerical workers and proprietors found their sons in jobs like their own or in other white collar pursuits. Special strains may have existed within the younger and older generations of working class families in Union Park, but across the generations there appeared some cause for the fathers to hope for a better station in life for their sons.

Work and the Forms of the Family

The impact of work on Union Park's families was not limited to these specific situations of strain between family members. Work also affected and was affected by the institution of the family as such. Because Union Park by 1880 had evolved so that the family unit was the only coherent primary group in the community, the interaction between urban work patterns and the family unit indicates something of how primary groups were fitted to the economic structure of the city.

THE FAMILY AS A GOAD TO WORK. The discrepancies in status to which blue collar brothers were subject were straightforward means by which the occupational structure of the city touched the lives of individual family members. But there was a more subtle, yet equally painful, possibility for the intervening of work in the lives of the young, to be seen in the experiences of newly married young men or middle aged men who failed to marry.

Married men in their twenties had the same patterns of occupational distribution as single men in their twenties. What was striking about the younger married worker was the stability of his employment. In the census-taking process for 1880, the census canvassers asked people whether or not they had been employed "continuously" during the preceding twelve-month period. This means of determining employment versus unemployment was singularly inexact, for those who had suffered a slight break in the process of changing jobs, and those who worked on a fee basis, were lumped together with men who were laid off temporarily or fired from jobs. Thus, in Union Park 93 percent of the executives in industries were continuously employed, but only 28 percent of the richest lawyers in the community were. In the white collar ranks during this prosperous year[2] curtailment of employment, by employers or by lack of trade, would probably have been overshadowed by changes of employment initiated by the employee himself. In any event, the measure of continuous employment the census takers made is useful now in determining those who were specially stable in their work; prominent among the specially stable workers were the young married men of Union Park.

The general pattern was that 39 percent of the single workers were continually employed, while 57 percent of the married were. The difference was greatest among the young. Of the married men in their early twenties, 61 percent were steadily employed during the year, while 36 percent of the single men of the same age were. In older age groups the gap between single and married workers narrowed, although the married group was always more stable than the single.

Since the pattern of job holding was the same for single and married young people, why did these differences appear? It is possible to imagine three social conditions, complementary to each other, that could account for these results in Union Park. Employers might have been less inclined to lay off or fire workers they knew to be married, so that employers were not considering their workers just as "a pair of hands" but as social creatures. Or second, married employees on the whole might have been better workers than single people; they had more at stake in the job, for they were responsible, through it, for the welfare of people besides themselves. This greater steadfastness in their work would of course have encouraged employers to retain them.

We have seen that a married couple with the husband

in his early or middle twenties was unusual; it was more typical for a man to wait a few years more until he had established himself in his vocation. This condition should have been connected to the usual job stability of the young married worker in a third way. The workers most anxious to establish themselves, most zealous in their work, should have been the young married men, who sensed themselves embarked on a somewhat unusual venture and who felt the need to get established, make their position especially secure, so that the timing of their marriage could be accounted or compensated for. The very need of these young married men to stabilize their lives and provide adequately for themselves, their wives, and their children may have meant they were unwilling or unable to experiment with a variety of employment, to take chances in order to make significant gains up the occupational ladder. The exceptional job stability they enjoyed during the year suggests, in other words, that exploratory capacities in work may have in fact been sharply limited for these people, more limited than those of young workers not yet committed to taking care of a marriage partner as well.

Young people living alone, a group composed mostly of young men, faced work as a different kind of goad. The problems of these young men were related to the fact that people who lived alone, of all ages, had a pattern of occupations diverging from those of other working adults who lived with someone else in a nuclear or extended family. The lone people of Union Park did not share the upper white collar strata to the degree other kinship groups did, because a much lower proportion of their numbers were proprietors of retail businesses. At the other end of the spectrum, they had a greater proportion of skilled blue collar workers in their midst than did the nuclear or extended family groups, though the same proportion of unskilled and semiskilled workers. Also to be found among these loners was a slightly greater proportion of clerical workers. In other words, their deprivation at one upper occupational level was compensated by a greater concentration at skilled manual labor and clerical work; these lone individuals had the least concentration at the bottom of the occupational structure, in unskilled labor.

Unlike the nuclear and extended families, whose workers were distributed across the decades of adulthood, the workers who lived alone were in the majority of cases young people between the ages of twenty and thirty. Most of these young people would eventually marry; for those who did not, who were over thirty but living alone in Union Park, their occupational profiles became increasingly unfavorable when compared to the profiles of workers in nuclear and extended families. Middle-aged workers living alone were much more concentrated in semiskilled trades than people in nuclear or extended families; while most of the breadwinners in nuclear or extended homes had moved out of clerical labor by the time they were in their middle forties, nearly a third of the people living alone remained in these occupations.

The capacity to form some kind of kin association during early adulthood thus was critical in avoiding a relative decline in status, such as these middle-aged single people experienced. To the loneliness of such a family situation for middle-aged men and women was thus joined an increasingly unfavorable economic outlook in comparison to those in Union Park who had married, or had forged a home with another relative. Whether or not young people understood this to be the case, the statistics, of course, cannot reveal. But the objective situation remained: those lone young people who had formed some kin alliance as they approached middle age were higher placed in work than the people who remained unmarried or without relatives to share their lives.

EMPLOYMENT AND FAMILY FORM. Almost all of the people living alone in Union Park worked. The real contrast in employment came between the two other main family groups, the nuclear and extended families. The contrast can be expressed as a difference in "work orientation" of the two family forms. Social psychologists use this term to denote a set of attitudes about work as well as the percentage of people in different types of households who do work. The Census reveals only the numbers of course; it measures the degree of participation in work by people in various kinds of families.[3]

In the forms of nuclear and extended families most prevalent in Union Park, those without boarders or servants, about 10 percent more of the family members were employed in the extended homes than the nuclear ones. Further, extended families were more work-oriented than nuclear families, not in the degree to which the heads of the respective families worked, but the degree to which other members worked: 87 percent of the heads of nuclear families worked, and 85 percent of family heads in extended families did; but while 17 percent of the other people in nuclear families worked, 34 percent of those in extended homes did. In most of these extended homes, where an "extra" relative lived with a married couple, it was the relative who worked, whether the extra person was a man or a woman. In only a twentieth of the extended families did the wife work and the extra person take care of the children.

The extent to which the work load was shared among family members was thus greater in the extended families of Union Park than in the nuclear ones. In the nuclear homes, encompassing most of the population of the community, the head of the family tended to be the sole provider, the person bearing economic responsibility for the fortunes of the family group. In this way the lesser work orientation among the nuclear family unit gave rise to a greater polarization of economic responsibility.

The question arises as to why these "extra" family members of the extended families in Union Park did work. After all, throughout the social spectrum most of the women in the dominant family form, the nuclear, did not work; why should not the extra kin of the extended homes, half of whom were women, have refrained as well? The common-sense answer would be that these extended families were poorer than the dominant family structure, and therefore more people in them had to work. And if extended families were poorer, then their small numbers in this prosperous Chicago community would also be explained, for this kinship type would somehow have been weeded out of Union Park. But the common-sense solution runs counter to one of the principal findings of this study, contained in the materials on the relation of the kinship system to the stratification of work.

Table 16 summarizes the relation between kinship and the occupational stratification of all workers in Union Park. The extended families did not, in this account, suffer in contrast to the nuclear forms; the distribution of occupation was, in fact, slightly "in favor" of the extended families. Poverty does not account for the greater work orientation of extended families. This can be seen in two other ways.

Among the heads of families in their forties and early fifties, those from extended homes were much more solidly white collar in their work than the heads of nuclear homes. The relative affluence of these two family groups

Table 16. The occupations of people in different family forms

	Type of family		
Occupational category	Single-member	Nuclear	Extended
High white collar			
Business	2.9%	4.9%	3.8%
Professional	3.5	5.7	7.2
Arts	2.7	3.9	3.0
Proprietary	6.3	11.1	12.8
Subtotal	15.4	25.6	26.8
Low white collar			
Business and government service (clerical)	27.8	22.1	19.2
Commercial service	17.7	17.2	23.0
Subtotal	45.5	39.3	42.2
Blue collar			
Highly skilled	3.6	3.2	3.8
Skilled	14.8	10.8	9.8
Manual semiskilled	6.9	7.0	5.0
Business and government semiskilled	6.7	6.4	5.7
Unskilled	3.4	4.5	3.8
Subtotal	35.4	31.9	28.1
Servant	3.5	3.1	3.0
Total	100	100	100
	N = 947	N = 4192	N = 521

could also be seen in the employment of servants. Among those extended families where the father was in his forties, 28 percent of the homes were able to employ a servant or servants; among nuclear families with fathers of the same age, 18 percent of the homes could afford servants. Thus, the nuclear family form, though dominant in the population of Union Park, did not favorably dominate the class stratification of this urban community. The superiority of its numbers did not imply also an economic superiority in 1880.

This situation in Union Park put to one test Parsons'

idea that nuclear families are functionally effective in terms of work and achievement in modern, dynamic societies, and for this reason have come to be the dominant mode of family organization. The family patterns of Union Park in 1880 confronted his theory at a more subtle level, as well.

The foreign-born workers of Union Park, as shown in Chapter Five, suffered inequality in the pattern of jobs they held when compared to the native-born in the community; these disadvantages were affected, in turn, by the nature of the family in which the foreigner lived. Table 17 shows this relation of occupation and family structure.

Table 17. Occupations of native- and foreign-born workers in three family types

	Single-member[a]	Nuclear[a]	Extended[a]
Occupation of native-born			
Executive or professional	9.2%	16.2%	17.3%
Proprietary	6.4	9.7	7.8
Clerical	49.8	41.4	44.1
Manual skilled	16.2	12.7	14.5
Manual unskilled	18.3	20.0	16.2
Total	100	100	100
	N = 592	N = 3797	N = 400
Occupation of foreign-born			
Executive or professional	8.4	10.2	7.0
Proprietary	6.3	14.8	23.3
Clerical	36.6	34.5	38.4
Manual skilled	23.5	17.2	11.6
Manual unskilled	25.2	23.4	19.8
Total	100	100	100
	N = 252	N = 1029	N = 149

[a] Without boarders or servants.

In Union Park in 1880 the foreign-born person living alone had a more inferior occupational position compared to his native-born counterpart than did the foreign individual in a nuclear family compared to his native-born counterpart. In the single-member families, the gap between native and foreigner widened; in the nuclear, it narrowed somewhat. Single-member families, as a whole, had a less favored occupational distribution than nuclear or extended families. Thus disabilities in Union Park tended to compound themselves: given one disability, foreign birth, its stratification pattern within another unfavored social form, the single-member family, intensified the disability.

But the category of extended families contained foreigners who were not at a disadvantage in work. Here differences between native and foreign manual laborers were ironed out to become almost equal. The native retained a slightly higher concentration of clerical labor; yet in the upper white collar groups, the foreigner had more then three times the percentage of proprietary owners than did the native-born, though less than half the executive and professional positions. This means that there was some correlation between the extended family form of organization, ethnicity, and the ability to own property-based business; a correlation also between this family form and the ability of the foreigner to reduce his numbers among the manually skilled.

Why or how the favored segment of the foreign-born population came to live in extended families, the data for this one year could not reveal. Yet, in itself, this material suggests that the nuclear families Parsons points to as functionally efficient in the society did not, in Union Park, shelter the groups of foreigners who had best coped with the disability of their birth in the work world; the extended families did.

Such fragments of evidence do not disprove the notions

of nuclear-family dominance advanced by Parsons and his followers. Rather, they suggest that in Union Park the reasons for the numerical dominance of nuclear families lay along different lines than the economic superiority this family form had in integrating family members into the work force of the city.

Family size, an equally important measure of privacy and shelter, also challenges the Parsonian notion. Among family leaders in their forties and early fifties, men heading large families of over six people constituted 13 percent of the executives of Union Park, though only 6 percent of the working population; men from small families of two people constituted 24 percent of the executives and 24 percent of the working population. For other family leaders in this age group, the trend was for the men in the larger families to be similarly better situated than men from small families. And at the very bottom of the occupational scale, there were to be found proportionately few middle-aged leaders of large families and many leaders of small families.

The social meaning of this material is twofold: there was first a limitation on the consequences of being poor, and second a privilege, better, a tangible reward, for those in the community who had attained a high status. Since the fact of poor occupational status evidently was antithetical to the development of very large families, a meager income was not in Union Park subjected to enormous family demands. This meant that for the least favored in the community, the family, in terms of its size, and the responsibilities attendant on its size, did not compound the miseries of being poor. One could argue that an unskilled laborer with two children felt the burden of his family responsibilities more heavily than a store owner with two children, but it could not be argued that the unskilled laborer was in addition more likely to have a larger brood than that of the store owner. Rather the reverse: the data show that the population maintained a certain balance so that those who were poor were more likely to concentrate at the other extreme of living alone, where the little they had could be conserved for themselves. This accords with the conclusion, already advanced, that family building took place in Union Park only after an economic base of security had been established by the worker.

But this formulation, while perhaps materially favoring the circumstances of the poor, ignores the emotional side of the issue. To be able to have a number of children, to enjoy them at different ages over a long period of time, to create a diverse and varied circle within the home, is a deeply gratifying experience. To be able to enjoy such richness of family life was, the data indicate, one of the concrete rewards of job success in Union Park; as a consequence of prosperity, there came the freedom to create and enjoy large and diverse families to an extent not practicable for people of lesser means.

The Hidden Unities

There was a hidden unity in the work experience of family members and family groups in Union Park. The strains in family balance and continuity caused by work, the goad of family responsibilities on the worker, and the effect of intensive conditions of family life on work achievement, all were bound together, I believe, by the position of the family as the only coherent primary group in the individual's relation to the immense, growing city of Chicago. The hypothesis I shall advance is that the family was used as the immediately available tool by which men such as those in Union Park tried to shield

141

themselves from the disorder and diversity of the city; it is this shielding process which explains the configurations of family and work in 1880.

To form a picture of the quality of experience embodied in these statistics on Union Park in 1880, it might be helpful to see what they would tell about a young man from Union Park working in the city during this year. Were he to come from a home where only his parents and siblings lived, he would have been nurtured, in almost all cases, in a milieu where his father had borne sole responsibility for the fortunes of the household, no matter how poor the family was. His mother remained at home to care for him and his brothers and sisters; he and the other children would have been shielded from working until they were in their seventeenth or eighteenth year, after a decade of schooling.

Were this young man to have come from a more complex home, an extended one, the operations of the household would have been less neatly divided. More of the adult generation would have been at work, and so a clear-cut division of labor between adults would not have existed to the degree it did in a nuclear home. While the child himself did not have to begin work any earlier than his counterpart in a nuclear home, his relations to the older people in the family were to people as a unit more concerned with what they did in the outside world, and less directly confined to the home.

Young men usually began their careers either as clerical workers or as skilled manual laborers; these were, indeed, the occupations of youth. What kinds of people would a young person mix with, if he entered one or the other of these pursuits? The census materials indicate that clerical occupations drew on young people from all classes of parents, so that clerical work was a kind of second-generation melting pot. The condition in skilled labor was somewhat the same, though parental backgrounds here were more weighted toward the skilled working class itself. Both of these jobs tended to expose a young man to a diversity of people, and might have acquainted him with a host of peer associates with whom perhaps he had not come into contact as a child. The shock of this obviously would have been specially great for those young workers who had been shielded from the city, through the intensive and private families that were the distinctive feature of the community. For the fathers of Union Park who were executives, this diversity of people their children encountered in work was more marked than in the other white-collar groups. There are theorists of social mobility who view this dispersion from the top ranks of the social order as an inevitable phenomenon; for the families involved in such a fall, however, they only knew it hurt.

Among the young men of Union Park, employment affected family life in two other ways, both involving young people who were "left behind" the majority of their fellows. Older brothers who were blue collar laborers were left behind their younger brothers, who for the most part were white collar employees.

Young people who lived alone into their thirties, who failed to marry or to establish some kind of living arrangement with a relative, were similarly left behind the young men who forged kinship alliances as they approached middle age. Middle-aged lone people were not, contrary to older theories of social mobility,[4] especially diverse in their job holding, for they retained a pattern of young adult work that was cast off by people who had developed kin associations as they matured. Forming an alliance or responsibility to someone else presumably gave a young man impetus to make something of himself. Both nuclear and extended family forms played a positive role in fostering this impulse and preventing a "freeze" at the young-adult stage of development. Perhaps family-making for these people was the logical rationale for a man's striving to better himself in the work world. If this was true, the release of aggression involved in competing with other men for a better place in the world found its "cover" in the good the results of this striving would bring to people other than the individual himself.[5]

It was the work experience of fathers and sons together, the experience of whole family units, that revealed most sharply the place of the family in the community and the city. In the simplest measurement of work among various family forms, the extended families of Union Park were more oriented to work, as family units, than the nuclear. When the distribution of jobs among different family forms was charted, the nuclear and extended forms showed little gross difference, but the census data when refined showed the extended family leaders in their forties to be better placed in work, and more able to afford such amenities as servants, than nuclear family leaders of a similar age. In the work experience of men in their forties leading small, compact families versus those leading larger ones, the same pattern emerged: the more complex, less concentrated family form possessed a higher position on the economic scale. Again, the extended family forms sheltered more of those who had overcome the occupational disadvantages of foreign birth than did the dominant order of nuclear families. The conditions of the extended home of 1880 in Union Park fit the requisites, along these lines, that modern writers like Lipset and Bendix single out as generally necessary for upward mobility of lower groups.[6]

This leads back to the argument between Ariès and Parsons. Why did the intensiveness and privacy of the families of Union Park stand out so sharply at the time, and what relation did the character of these families have to the work life of the city? The measures of intensity of family life through formal structure, following Ariès and Parsons, the measures of such other elements as family size, and the stages of maturation all suggest that this dominance of intensive family life was not explicable along the lines of adaptation to entrepreneurial and large-scale bureaucratic life, as Parsons would have it. The dominant family forms and structures did not owe their numbers to some superior functioning in the work world, when compared to a minority form like the extended family; in this one community at this one point in time, Parsons' argument is inadequate to piece together the relations between family and work.

There is an equal problem in relation to Ariès' argument, for he explains how intense families might have sheltered children and limited the range of the whole family's experience, but he does not explain why this kind of family was so prevalent, why the nuclear family was still the dominant mode of life for middle class people such as these. Ariès' critique of the nuclear family may be correct, but his argument cannot explain the power of family life in Union Park. The materials from the 1880 Census, however, suggest a uniquely urban situation to which the families of Union Park responded.

One quality unified four seemingly unrelated social conditions in this community. The first of these was that the stages of family life past childhood, but before middle age in the forties, were unstructured in the manner in which breaks from the parental home were accomplished. Secondly, there was a greater tendency for work stability among the youngest people who had married than among the same age group who had not married. This stability may have meant that the burdens of early marriage were such that young married men could not afford to take chances by changing jobs as often as young men who were still unattached. Third, an unequal rate of employment of women in the upper and lower classes was related to the fact that the wives of working men tended to have better jobs than their husbands, and so, to permit the husband to remain the leader in the family, the wives were prohibited or prohibited themselves from working. Fourth, the pattern of life stages made plausible Ariès' description of the nuclear family as an isolating unit in the society, an institution whose purpose and scope was to create a shelter for certain of its members from the larger society.

The emotional element that bound these four social conditions together was fear. A confused passage from one's parents' home to a home of one's own should have created fear about what was happening; there was no clear communal pattern to refer to, and unlike the older farm or village, the options for choice and for error in this immense city must have been so great as to be overwhelming. For a person in transit between the family of his parents and a family of his own, the lack of a common means of transition could only have produced anxiety about how one was to work the matter out.

If one married very young, fear about what would happen to the family must have been greater than for people who waited to marry until they were established in the work world. Youthful marriage might therefore have fostered a desire to insure success by hewing steadily to the same job, by avoiding chancy positions, risky new ventures. The satisfaction of being married as soon as one was an adult thus became counterbalanced by the evident will to make the family stable, to sustain it by steadily working away at the job. In the midst of a city growing at a rapid rate, where businesses failed as often as they succeeded, where bureaucratic rules for advancement were not standardized, where, in short, entrepreneurial dynamism was characteristic of the city's life as a whole, a very young, married worker was not free to explore the way other people were.

Prohibiting one's wife from working because she may upset the lines of authority in the house by having a better job, paying more money, even though the family needed that money, was also a clear case of fear. Economics were sacrificed for a sense of secure marital identity in which a husband was able to show a clear power in the work world, a power that placed him and justified him in the family circle.

Would it not be reasonable, with such tangible signs of fear about work, that the place of the family would be that of a defensive refuge from the work world? A well-articulated secondary literature now exists about the fear, in general, that people of the time had of cities; surely the family played a specific role in the expression of this fear.[7] The upbringing of children in such a society would not focus on their participation in the city. Nor would the husband and wife turn to the community for social activity. Rather, the family would become the instrument of defense against the increasing complexity and uncertainty of the city environs. The family would thus become a retreat from perceived disorder.

It is logical that intensive forms of the family should have predominated, for they, on the account of Ariès and the census data, provided the greatest shelter from the social character of the city work world at large. The intensive family was a private, personal unit; the structure of work was becoming increasingly impersonal, organized in large offices, shops, and factories. The division of labor in the intensive family was clear-cut, but even more important, it was for a long period permanent: the child as a child never acted like a father to his father, nor the wife, in 93 percent of the cases, like a breadwinner to her children. Contrast this to the shifting character of the division of labor in the work force, where as social mobility or job change occurs, the worker acquires new roles and tasks, new senses of what he is.

Rapid increase in the numbers of people in this city, and of the bureaucracies which serviced their needs and employed them, could have been counteracted by a sense of family in which the family molded itself as the mirror opposite of disorder and complexity in the city. The structure of the intensive family, through nucleation, small size, binding of the young adult life stages to the home, was more fitted to foster and strengthen this defensive reaction than was the structure of "looser" families; yet, it could not be argued that people in less intensive families were a priori more purposefully adaptive to the city, more purposefully explorative and less defensive. The structures, rather, of these less intensive families fostered a socialization network by weakening the structural circumstances under which a defensive isolation could sustain itself.

In this way the strength of the intensive family was a direct outcome of the dialogue between the individual and the forces that were urbanizing him. The family was his means of preserving a small, intimate pattern of human association and control that he was unable to maintain in the city, as might have been possible "in the old days" on the farm or in the small town. An increasing body of research is showing that Sorokin's famous theory of urbanization as involving a transformation from extended to nuclear family units is misleading, in that significant patterns of nuclear family forms existed in preindustrial, rural, or semirural areas.[8] But the importance of this overwhelming nucleation of family life in Union Park was not in what it indicated about the origin of the nuclear form, but the use made by city people of the nuclear family, the small family, or the family in which life stages were bound to one intimate situation. The process of urbanization in this Chicago community meant the intensive family came to have a unique purpose of its own in relation to the city, as a defense mechanism roping in the child's experience and broad human understanding, by shielding him until young adulthood from the metropolis and its work force.

The context of life for these middle class people was a sort of great if inarticulate battle, between the forces of fear centered in the intimate, isolated family and the chaotic, ruthless vigor of the industrial and bureaucratic work order of this new metropolis. The fathers of Union Park were the men caught in the middle of the battle. To understand them truly, and the other puzzles of Union Park's family structure, it is necessary to explore the outcome of this hypothesis, the outcome of the battle between the families of Union Park and the work order of Chicago over the course of two decades.

Part Three

SOCIAL MOBILITY AND

INTENSE FAMILY LIFE

8

TRACING FAMILIES

Of all groups in nineteenth century America, the urban middle classes should have been especially successful in coping with the emerging industrial order. Their fortunes were not tied to land, nor were they yoked to the exhausting physical labor of the factory; instead they worked in the city offices, banks, and stores that were gradually acquiring a dominant role in the economy of the country. To them, if anyone, must surely have belonged the vigor and exploratory spirit associated with the rise of the giant industrial cities.

Yet, the lives of people in the Chicago community of Union Park point in a different direction. The interweaving of family and work in the census year 1880 was such that it would be difficult to explain the presence of intense, sheltered families in the community because they were associated with superior advantages in the work world, a confluence supposed in the influential theory of Talcott Parsons. Instead, the structure of the Union Park community in 1880 suggests that the dominant mode of family life may have owed its existence to forces apart from, even in opposition to, the efficient integration of family members to the city's work force.

This line of reasoning offers clues, but does not explain,

the puzzle contained in the conventional documents of Union Park's history: why the families during Union Park's bourgeois era evidenced a different relation between husband and wife than that to be found when the district was an elite suburb, and what role work, and mobility in work, played in determining the relations between middle class husbands and wives, fathers and sons.

The results of a trace of one thousand fathers and sons from 1872 to 1890 provide materials for solving this puzzle; it is in this long-term trace that the issues suggested in the intensive analysis of family and work in 1880 are made clear. This trace involved selecting all the families in the 1880 Census where a father, or occasionally a lone mother had a son at work; the heads of these families and the working sons were located when possible in directories of the City of Chicago in two-year steps back to 1872 and forward to 1890. Thus it was possible to sketch the occupational and residential history of these families and compare the generations.

The tracking down of these thousand Union Park people revealed, for the majority of families, that the family became a refuge for fathers who were in fact stagnant in their work, even though the economic structure of Chicago was rapidly expanding. In this stagnation, this lack of vigor, whose surface character was noted in Union Park at the time, lay the origins of a condition that has, on many accounts, persisted into the present: a special weakness of middle-class fathers in relation to their sons, and a consequent sense of family in which the mother is taken as the strong force; in Union Park occurred, in other words, a failure of middle class fatherhood, where the father was unable, due to his own work experience, to prepare his children to cope with the urban society in which they would live.

Conducting the Trace

The design of the tracing had a simple form: the occupation and residence of people in certain 1880 family groups were mapped for the even-numbered years from 1872 to 1890; the type of family in 1880 was taken, for reasons explained below, as a "given," a fixed indicator of family structure. The fixed qualities included family form and size, the sex and ethnic background of the family leader, the number of sons in the family in 1880. Changes in work and residence were traced separately for each generation for the eighteen-year period.

The explanation for this design lies largely in the materials available for a long-term study. The only good census materials of the period available now to a researcher are those of the 1880 Census. Records from 1870 were fragmentary for Chicago, and most of the 1890 Census materials for the city burned in a fire at the Treasury Department in 1924. Materials from the 1900 Census are not available at this time for academic research. Thus it would be almost impossible to trace the people of Union Park back or forward in time through the complete population mapping that occurs during the decennial census. Further, ten years is a long time, and much could have happened within that time that would be obscured or lost through comparing a situation at the beginning of one decade with its state ten years later. Some other source was needed, one that would provide coherent social information for the Union Park families at frequent intervals.

These requirements eliminated much of the standard matter on which historians rely. Property records, marriage licenses, and the like were excluded, since not everyone bought property or married during the time of trace;

church records were similarly unusable, since many people in cities at this time did not belong to churches; voting lists covered the populace extensively but contained very little information on occupation or family. The records that most nearly satisfied the requirements of extensive population coverage, short, regular time units, and adequate social information were directories of the city, privately printed guides listing the residents of the city of Chicago, their addresses, and their occupations. These annual directories gave information on the men at work in the city, and on women when they were heads of household. While there was a tendency not to list people at the very bottom of society, "respectable" unskilled laborers were listed. For prosperous working class and middle class groups in Chicago such as the people of Union Park, the mapping of the city directories was the most extensive of all available documents. Annual publication meant the directories met the time-span requirement very well; and the standard listing of occupation and address made this material ideally suited to tracking down the mobility in status and residence of families with distinctive characteristics in the 1880 Census.

The process sounds simple when expressed verbally, but in fact contains some hidden problems. First, the actual number of individuals traced in the city directories could not be as large as the total number of sons and fathers at work in Union Park in 1880. The reason for this was the virtual impossibility of tracing people with names like Jones or Smith once they had changed their 1880 address. No precise formula for determining what constituted a "common" name was used in the study; only the most obvious problems were eliminated from the sample.

After this process of elimination, the sample totaled 1040 individuals: 423 heads of household; 422 first sons (eldest if more than one in family worked); 148 second sons; 36 third sons; and 11 fourth sons. These individuals constituted more than one twelfth the population of Union Park and one sixth of the working population; they were members of families that altogether totaled about 2400 persons, or a sixth of the census population.

About 60 percent of the family members in each generation could be located in the city directories for at least one year other than 1880, as is shown in Table 18. On the

Table 18. Traceable individuals in each generation[a]

	Total in sample	Number traceable
Heads of household	423	255
First sons	422	250
Second sons	148	90
Third sons	36	22
Total	1029	617

[a] Number of fourth sons in sample was too small to be usably traced.

surface this 60 percent might appear to be the minimally stable urban element, and the untraceable 40 percent the transitory urbanites of Union Park. However, as indicated above, the people were traced only in even-numbered years. The use of alternate years, dictated by the amount of labor the trace entails, meant that there could have been loophole migration. For example, a family could have been in Chicago three years, from 1879 to 1881, which would be as "stable" a residence as someone listed from 1878 to 1880, and yet be missed.[1]

There is in any distributive tracing of this sort the problem of "selective attrition," where people who are very downwardly mobile, or in the midst of severe personal problems, or in trouble with the law, move away from an inhospitable place. To the extent such misfits lived at the lower echelons of society they would not have interfered with a tracing procedure in the Union Park neighborhood to the degree they might in a community located in a slum or factory-workers' area.

The city directories, I have noted, had a class bias, so that people at the very bottom of the social scale were excluded. How did this bias affect the histories used for the Union Park families? Test comparison of the listings of the city directory of 1880 with the listings of the Census shows some inaccuracy in four of fifty cases where the occupation of the person traced was white collar, and eleven of fifty cases where the occupation was lowest-grade manual labor.

The trace population was, however, the solid and established sector of the community. As Table 19 shows, it was a more white collar, more prosperous group than the population as a whole, even if the unequal numbers of people in the "not employed" category were removed and the percentages redistributed. In addition, it had a slightly greater concentration of men than the general population. It had the same concentration of nuclear families; all the other families were, of necessity, extended, instead of evenly divided between single-member and extended. The trace population had a much greater concentration of larger families, and a greater concentration of foreign-born family heads.

There are statistical means by which to correct somewhat the skewing of the trace population in terms of the Census population. For example, measures of occupational change in different ethnic groups can treat native and foreign-born groups as separate populations; one can compute occupational percentages within each group, and then compare changes in percentage patterns between the two groups. In this way, the developmental qualities of the

Table 19. Social characteristics of trace sample and general population in 1880

Trait	Trace	General population
Sex of household head		
Male	79%	84%
Female	21	17
Kinship type of all individuals		
Nuclear	79	80
Extended	21	10
Family size		
2–4	43	53
5–6	34	14
7–11	23	6
Nativity of head		
U. S.	58	67
Foreign	43	33
Occupation		
Professional or executive		6[a]
Head	14	
First son	12	
Second son	5	
Proprietor		5
Head	14	
First son	8	
Second son	10	
Clerical		19[b]
Head	22	
Eldest son	50	
Second son	54	
Skilled manual		11
Head	20	
Eldest son	22	
Second son	20	
Unskilled		10[c]
Head	4	
Eldest son	8	
Second son	11	
Not employed		49
Head	26	
Eldest son	none	
Second son	none	

[a] Includes the arts on 1880 scale.
[b] Includes clerks for businesses and government and commercial service on 1880 scale.
[c] Includes servants.

variables that differed in the trace sample and the general population are not wholly transformed by changes in relative concentration.

The Nontraceables

We have seen that about 61 percent of the trace sample could be located in the city directories; 39 percent could not. What were the differences between the transitory minority and the more rooted majority?

The list of differences have no clear order. More of the women heads of household tended to be untraceable than men (44 percent women untraceable versus 38 percent men). Among eldest sons, the youngest and the oldest age groups were more untraceable (49 percent and 44 percent respectively) than sons from 20 to 25 years old (33 percent untraceable). Among second sons, those under 20 were more untraceable than those who were adults (49 percent versus 35 percent). Fathers tended to be between the ages of 45 and 55; women who were traceable tended to cluster in the same age grouping.

Workers from nuclear families were less traceable than those from extended families (42 percent untraceable versus 28 percent); there seemed, however, to be little difference between families of different size in their traceability. Ethnicity did seem to play a role in how stable the population was to the city, with the foreign-born family heads being less traceable than the native-born (44 percent to 35 percent). Among heads of families, the rate of untraceability generally increased the lower the person was on the occupational scale, though there were too few unskilled workers to judge at this level; among the sons, there was no clear correlation between traceability and occupational class. Similarly, the number of sons in a family did not seem to bear on the traceability of the individuals in the family.

Interpretive Problems in the Trace Data

The census sample for this study was large, as community studies go: 12,000 people for whom individual, standardized records were available. Furthermore, the character of the census mapping was geographically complete. There was no sampling of the population of various areas, but inclusion, rather, of all the individuals and families who resided in the mapped areas. This satisfying character of the 1880 data may spoil the reader's taste for the trace data. Instead of tables of two or three thousand individuals, the numbers here are in the hundreds, and statistical indicators of these small groups, percentage computations, may seem misleading when contrasted to the previous populations on which percentages were computed. This is a problem which generally afflicts studies of mobility between generations: it appears to be difficult to obtain large samples.

The low number of cases in some of the tables derived from the trace data prompts an attempt to close the "credibility gap" that attends measures with a low numerical base. The means by which this difficulty has been in part surmounted relates, though, to another problem involved in the compilation of the data from the city directories.

It should be evident that the terms of this trace could not be limited to individuals who could be consecutively located backward or forward in time from 1880. In-and-out migration is for all large urban communities, especially during developmental phases, too important a population movement to be excluded. Yet if one simply consulted the directories year after year, coding individuals whenever they were found in the city, a certain kind of distortion could result. Nuclear and extended families, for example, had about equivalent concentration levels in the trace sample for most years. This does not mean the same families resided in the city throughout this period, but that the in-and-out migration of these two family forms balances in such a way that their relative concentration remained constant over time. In other words, the social character of the population, as defined by this one variable, might have been the same over time, but the actual individuals themselves need not have been.

This difficulty, and the problems of different trace patterns of various social traits, and of the relatively low numbers of the trace sample, are dealt with in two ways. There are employed, first, measures of the experience of individuals, so that, for example, a measure was made of how many people who were clerks in 1880 had become store owners by 1890. This was a measure of what is called here linked change, and the number of people who could be so traced over long periods tended to be low. An alternative kind of population measurement, distributional change, deals with a fairly sizeable population. As a counterpart to the example above, in making a measure of the distributional change of clerks from 1880 to 1890, the percentage of clerks in the working population in 1880 was compared to the percentage of clerks in 1890. If in 1890 there were half as many clerks in the working population as in 1880, one has described the composite history of a class of individuals. This is different in kind from describing how many clerks in 1880 were clerks in 1890. In the direct, linked description of change the level of analysis was concrete individuals; in the composite, distributional description of change, the level of analysis was the class or social form as a phenomenon in and of itself.

This distributional approach is one statistical expression of Emile Durkheim's argument for social characteristics having a uniqueness of their own, apart from the lives of the separate individuals who compose the social group. The difference between the measures of linked and distributional change was not then simply in the size of the usable statistical sample, but in the kind of phenomenon described. In analyzing the trace sample measures on the direct level and on the Durkheimian distributional level have been compared to each other and used in conjunction in order to present as complex a portrait as possible of the process of historical change for individuals and social groups in Union Park.

9

THE SOCIAL MOBILITY

OF TWO GENERATIONS

Of all the elements of family life in Union Park whose meaning was withheld from the casual glances of outsiders, none was more hidden, nor more significant, than changes in work and residence of these families. The shape of mobility in work and residence was drawn by the nature of the families themselves; their intensity, as measured by family size and form, determined the kind of experience the Union Park family members had in the city at large.

It would be easy to assume that changes in job or residence for Union Park families meant they were experiencing a significant shift socially, and that the absence of change somehow counted for less in their lives. But the common sense of the matter is misleading. In the United States after the Civil War, the expectation and demographic reality was for rapid change in terms of where people lived; similarly, the self-help and success ideologies of the time picture job movement to be almost routine.[1] With change the order of the day, the existence of residential and occupational immobility, such as appeared in Union Park, was specially significant; the problem of this stability was whether it resulted from an unusually strong position of these people in society, or from forces of stagnation and an inability to respond to the dynamism of the larger culture.

Change and stability are relative terms, and require a standard of comparison. Fortunately, the social mobility of the Union Park people did offer an internal standard. There were striking differences in job and residence mobility between the dominant family configurations in Union Park and the family configurations shared by only a minority of its population. These differences, between nuclear and extended families, between small and large families, cast the intense modes of family life, the small homes, the nuclear homes, in a somber light.

First Set of Findings: Family Size and Mobility in Work

Both fathers and sons in large families were upwardly mobile to a greater degree than the same generations in small families.

The Census of 1880 showed that most families in Union Park were composed of between two and six kin. A majority of the population lived in homes of four or less, with the remainder living in families of five or six, and only occasionally in larger family units. In 1880, for family leaders of similar ages the men from larger families tended to be a little more favorably placed on the socio-economic ladder. The data from family tracing showed that this same pattern extended over the course of the following decade; yet, in the years before 1880, men from small (2–4 kin) and large (5–6 kin) families started from quite similar occupational backgrounds. Thus from a fairly equal starting point, the fathers of large families achieved a greater degree of upward mobility than the fathers of small homes. In the second generation this pattern was repeated, so that sons from small and large homes, beginning work in similar ways, gradually acquired a much different work experience.

From an occupational base in 1872 and 1876 somewhat similar to that of small families, leaders from the large families became solidly white collar as a group; by 1890 nearly a third of them were executives and professionals, and virtually none were manual laborers. Yet the smaller family leaders retained a level of 25 to 27 percent manual laborers — actually, the level of unskilled labor among these men rose a little over the course of time. The leaders of small families, in fact, changed their distribution of occupations very little over the course of the eighteen-year period. In the midst of the enormous growth in white collar administrative and commercial occupations in Chicago, they remained fairly static in their general patterns of job holding.

The leaders of the sprinkling of very large families had a mixed pattern of occupational mobility over the course of the eighteen years from 1872 to 1890. They started more favorably placed on the occupational scale in the 1870's but experienced increases in manual labor in the 1880's that offset their increasing proportion of executives and professionals. This group of fathers from unusually large families was in addition of slightly older average age than the men from large or small families, who clustered in the age group of the late forties in 1880.

More dramatic changes were to be found in the sons of these three different kinds of families. Graph 1 shows what the pattern of occupation of eldest sons in these families was in 1876 compared to 1890. Over the course of fourteen years, the concentration of sons from small families in manual labor increased by 9 percent, and

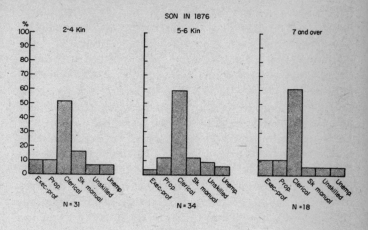

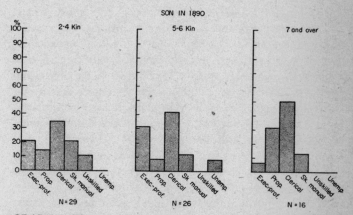

GRAPH 1. The occupations of eldest sons in 1876 and 1890, by family size

declined in the group of sons from large (5–6 kin) families by an equal amount. While the percentage of those sons from small families who were executives and professionals increased by 11 points, it increased 28 points for sons from the larger families. Sons from exceptionally large homes had a pattern of employment over the course of these years whose final effect was similar to that of sons from the large families. In all three cases, clerical work was in 1876 the starting occupation of the majority of the young, from which they fanned out as they grew older.

The direct tracing for a decade of all those who were clerical workers in 1880, both fathers and sons, explains something further of the mobility processes revealed here. The direct tracing is shown in Graph 2. Whereas about 25 percent of clerical workers from small families were downwardly mobile into manual labor over the decade, only 3 percent from the larger families were; there were no instances of such downward mobility among clerical workers from exceptionally large families. The movement in the larger families was coherently upward, in the smaller families it was scattered. At the very top of the occupational ladder, in executive and professional work, those from small families in 1880 were able to remain executives to a much more limited extent over the course of the decade (44 percent of the executives from small families in 1880 were executives in 1890) than large families (75 percent remained executives from 1880 to 1890) or in exceptionally large families (86 percent remained executives over the course of the decade.)

The social question in these findings on mobility is why family size should have mattered at all. In the 1870's families of different size had a fairly equal "start" in their occupational distribution and yet the smaller families suffered, in both generations, over the course of time. In these smaller families, family leaders were static in their job holdings compared to family leaders of similar age in larger homes; the sons from small families were ex-

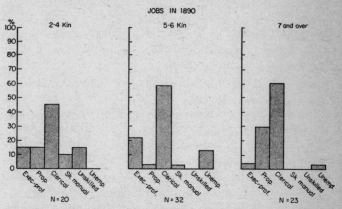

GRAPH 2. The occupations in 1890 of men who were clerical workers in 1880, by family size

periencing downward mobility to a degree that sons from larger families did not experience, though both groups of sons began the same. When the occupational history of classes of workers was traced directly, rather than distributionally, the same disability and relative downward mobility of workers from small families was revealed. It seems logical, then, that something was involved in the family process of the small homes not present, or different from, the processes at work in larger homes. These tighter, less diverse families were evidently caught up in a situation that did not equip them to deal with the expanding work order of Chicago as the other families could.

What is so striking about these trace materials is that the same pattern prevailed when the intense, nuclear families were matched against the more diverse, extended homes of Union Park.

Second Set of Findings: Family Form and Mobility in Work

The fathers and sons in extended families were more upwardly mobile in their jobs than fathers and sons in nuclear families.

The clearest place to begin with these findings is in occupation shifts among the population of eldest sons from nuclear and extended homes. In 1876 the occupational distribution of sons in nuclear and extended families had the same dominant trait: a majority were clerical workers, and each of the other occupations employed 12 percent or under of the family groups. Ten years later, the distribution was much different, as is shown in Graph 3. Almost as many nuclear-family sons were clerks as before; there occurred a 9 percent increase in the numbers employed in higher status jobs, and a 1 percent decline in manual labor. In the extended families, the percentage engaged in clerical labor dropped twenty points and increased twenty-six points in higher status jobs. During this decade, the whole class of unskilled laborers disappeared from the group of extended family sons.

The situation four years later, in 1890, solidified the changes that emerged in the decade between 1876 and 1886. Among these eldest sons of nuclear families, the concentration of clerical laborers dropped more sharply in these four years than in the previous ten, but there was only a 4 percent increase into higher white collar occupations, and a similar 4 percent increase in the concentration of blue collar laborers, mostly at the level of unskilled labor. Among eldest sons of extended families, the con-

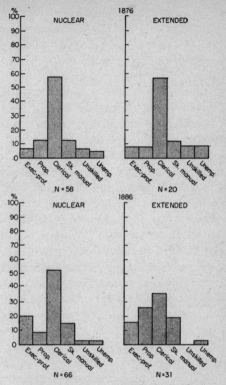

GRAPH 3. The occupations of eldest sons in 1876 and 1886, by type of family

centration of clerical laborers held firm, with a further increase in the upper white collar positions and a drop in the concentration of the blue collar positions.

If the extended-family sons in 1890 are compared with the nuclear-family sons in 1890, given that both groups started fourteen years earlier with a similar occupational profile, it is striking how much greater their gains were. A large concentration of proprietors in the extended-family sons' ranks had been achieved, compared to the nuclear group, with a fair similarity in concentration of executives and professionals: in all, 45 percent of the extended-family sons occupied these two upper ranks while only 32 percent of the nuclear-family sons did. In lower job groups, the sons from extended families were less concentrated in both clerical work and skilled labor than the sons from nuclear families, and had wholly ceased to perform unskilled labor. The extended-family sons in 1890 were thus more solidly white collar, and within that designation more concentrated at the upper levels of white collar work.

It might seem easy to explain these mobility patterns in terms of family economics, for, after all, there were more working adults in the extended family homes, and so there ought to have been more money to launch youngsters into the world. The weakness of this economic explanation is twofold. Sons from extended families started in roughly the same occupation pattern as sons from nuclear families; were the economics of the family wholly responsible for the mobility patterns, we would expect a different distribution between the two groups, especially at the outset of a career, when the young would most have needed help, either as capital from the father or placement through the father's influence in a good job. This argument applied equally to the emergent differences between sons in large and small families. Something else about these families, apart from their money resources, must have been at work to create this particular mobility pattern. Secondly, although sons classed as proprietors included young men working in stores owned by their families, the large percentage of extended-family sons classed as proprietors cannot be explained simply as the incorporation of the younger generation in the family business. This was, as will be shown in Graph 4, because there was a lower and steadily declining concentration of fathers from extended families who were proprietors compared to nuclear-family heads owning stores.

There is an important parallel between the work lives of the sons and of their fathers in these two family forms. When the fathers in the two family groups are compared early in their careers, the patterns of job holding are similar. This was true for their sons as well. But the fathers, as a whole, are evenly spread throughout the occupational spectrum in 1872, whereas the sons, as a whole, were concentrated in clerical labor, when we first analyzed their careers in 1880. Why did the fathers, eight years earlier, show this even spread throughout the job spectrum?

Before the Civil War, Chicago was more a town than a metropolis; there occurred growth in population and commerce during the years between the Civil War and the Fire of 1871, but the character of Chicago was still that of a provincial outpost, burgeoning though it was. Then, during the years with which this study is concerned, Chicago changed suddenly and radically. From the Great Fire to the opening of the present century, Chicago's population doubled every ten years; this massive number of people was increasingly engaged in a kind of commerce unknown in the towns and small cities of the early Republic, commerce that was national in its scope, with large numbers of workers in each company arranged in hierarchical positions of authority, defined by a manager or group of trustees at the top of the labor structure. These new industries were, in fact, so large as to require large secondary staffs of administrators, plus a rapidly growing service group, auxiliary to the actual productive activities in the plant. As Reinhardt Bendix has shown so well, the striking character of American urban industrialism during this era was not the simple rise in productivity through large-scale manufacturing, but the sudden growth of an immense bureaucratic machinery to staff and service the productive components in the factories. Thus did large towns become, economically, cities.[2]

Chicago was uniquely situated to participate in the growth of industrial bureaucracy along with the growth of factories. Its geography made it the logical center for communication and transfer in nationwide enterprises like meatpacking and steel; its geography, again, made it the logical depot and marketing point for regional industries, like flour milled in the upper Midwest, or for centralized capital resources, through its large banking resources. In the town of Chicago that existed before the Great Fire, such transfer, market, and communication activities were present, but not on the scale, and not involving as much a percentage of the city's labor force, as came to be true in the twenty years after the Fire.[3]

Thus the undifferentiated work characteristics between different families in the early and the middle 1870's occurred in an economy lacking as yet a labor structure involving large impersonal enterprises organized along hierarchic, bureaucratic lines. But as the structure of work evolved along new lines and became bureaucratized, family differences in work did emerge. In this way, the differences in family form or size were measures of the sensitivity of the Union Park homes to a profound change in the structure of urban society: these emerging family differences tell what shapes of family life were responsive to the bureaucratization of work in the city.

By 1876, labor patterns among the leaders of nuclear

and extended families began to show signs of divergence. There was a rise in the concentration of executives and professionals in the extended-family group from what existed in 1872, so that proportionately more executives were heads of extended families than heads of nuclear families. On the other hand, the same proportion of nuclear-family leaders were proprietors in 1876 as in 1872, and the level of extended-family proprietors dropped somewhat during these four years.

The direction of growth in these two white collar categories continued over the course of the next decade. By 1886 the nuclear-family heads maintained their concentration as proprietors while the extended-family leaders dropped again in the numbers who ran stores, but remained slightly more concentrated in the executive and professional group. As shown in Graph 4, this growth direction had achieved a definite form by 1890: proportionately twice as many nuclear-family heads were engaged as proprietors than extended-family heads, while the extended-family heads had now greater concentration in executive posts and the professions.

The long-term changes in lower classes were as follows: there was a 17 percent drop in the manual labor force of the extended-family head. The concentration of clerical labor in the extended-family group steadily increased with this decline of skilled and unskilled labor. In the group of nuclear-family leaders, skilled and unskilled labor remained at almost the same levels over the course of eighteen years.

These complicated patterns add up to three social conditions. The first is that sons did not, in either family form, follow in their fathers' footsteps, but had a peculiar occupational pattern of their own. Second, the sons from

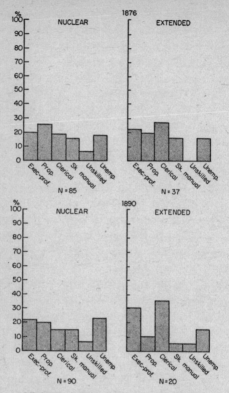

GRAPH 4. The occupations of family
head, 1876 and 1890, by type of family

extended families had a more favorable work experience
than sons from nuclear ones. Third, fathers from extended
families had a more favorable occupational history than
fathers from nuclear families. This third phenomenon
had a special character. The heads of nuclear families
were static as a group compared to extended-family lead-

ers. The extended-family fathers became over the course of time solidly white collar, while the nuclear-family fathers maintained the diverse distribution of white and blue collar jobs that characterized them in the year after the Great Fire.

These are the group or "distributional" phenomena. When we look at the "linked" changes — the changes in job for that smaller group of workers who remained in the city a decade — a further difference between nuclear family workers and workers from extended families is evident. Of the skilled workers in extended families in 1880, only 25 percent remained in manual labor in 1890; the rest moved up into the white collar classes. Fifty-two percent of the skilled workers in nuclear families in 1880, however, remained skilled workers a decade later. At the other end of the occupational scale, the data show that almost all of the executives from extended families were able to maintain their positions over the course of the decade, while only slightly more than half of the executives from nuclear families were able to do so.

The pattern of these statistics becomes more sharply defined when they are joined to the data on family size and mobility.

Some Conclusions from the Findings on Family Intensity and Work

Family size and family form were two elements of Union Park homes that seemed, on the evidence of the 1880 Census, to be bound up with the qualities of intensity and isolation observers remarked in the community. The results of tracing families in terms of these two traits strengthened the census evidence in a remarkable way.

Families of small size produced work patterns in both generations similar to families of nuclear form; families of large size produced patterns similar to families of extended form.

This confluence in tracing patterns revealed something deeper still about the Union Park families. In those homes where small size or nuclear form existed in 1880, the fathers seemed static as a group in their work patterns over the course of the eighteen years between 1872 and 1890. The fathers in less intensive family situations, by contrast, were more upwardly mobile over the course of time, and became a solidly white collar group. Sons from intensive families, that is families of small size and nuclear form, had a markedly less favorable work experience than sons from less intensive families; in addition, for all working members of the two kinds of families, those in the intensive families appeared to have a weaker grasp on the upper-status jobs they managed to have in 1880 over the course of the next decade. Lower down on the occupational scale of 1880, workers from intensive families had more difficulty moving upward than their counterparts in the other family situation. What is striking about these findings is that both of the family types began at similar points in the work world, and diverged as the city itself underwent a massive transformation in the organization of work. It appears, from this data, that large or extended families were better able to adapt to the emerging bureaucratic order of work in the city than the families constituting a majority in Union Park, of a more intense and isolated nature.

Why this should have been is explored in the final chapters of this study. But one implication of these findings emerged directly from the data: in the intensive families the fathers did not exhibit to the sons a pattern or a model of successful adaptation to work in the way that was present in the other homes. The sons seemed in turn to have suffered for it, the evidence suggests, since in the intensive families these young people had difficulty in keeping themselves in the white collar sphere, or successful within it, in a way sons from less intensive families did not.

In sum, if the role for a father in the middle class family was to induct and guide youths from the shelter of the home into the dynamism of the new industrial order, the fathers of intensive families in this particular middle class community had relatively little to pass on from their own experience. These fathers remained static in the face of the greatest urban changes; they seemed to have taken shelter themselves, in the midst of this restructuring of work, by doing the jobs they had always done. Their sons, who were not immobile, had no patterns of achievement to lean on, no fatherly model to guide them in their own careers, so that they, unlike the sons of a family form in which the fathers were dynamic, often fell into manual laboring positions or failed to maintain for good the upper status positions they at one time achieved. Surely, the ills of the intensive family, as Ariès describes them, were seen here as a most dramatic form. Why they happened seemed in Union Park related to generation differences Ariès did not envision. The places families lived showed this inner complexity of the generations even more strongly.

Third Set of Findings: Family Intensity and Rootedness to the Community

Whereas the heads of all families had somewhat similar patterns of residence, the sons of less intense families were much more mobile, geographically, than sons of intensive families.

Three different types of residence were used in the trace of the Union Park people: residence within the forty-square-block area of Union Park where Census manuscripts for 1880 were coded, residence in contiguous areas to this land mass that possessed the same social character, and residence in other parts of Chicago. These are crude divisions, but to have split the city into ten or twelve different regions would have made the numbers in each residence category unusably low.[4]

During the whole eighteen-year period of tracing, the leaders of families in Union Park showed little internal differences, along lines either of kinship form or of family size, in the patterns of their residence. There were some differences in nuclear and extended families in the years before 1880 as to whether the family leaders lived in Union Park itself or surrounding areas, but in general these families were long-term residents, not transitory dwellers in the neighborhood: nearly 80 percent of them had lived in the community or its environs since 1872.

In the decade of the 1880's, when Union Park was beginning to lose its "desirability," the family leaders showed a remarkable steadfastness in residence. Two thirds of the leaders of families of all types who resided in or near Union Park in 1880 still lived there in 1890. For all groups of family heads there was relatively little movement away from the whole of this area of Chicago; such migrations as occurred were within the near West Side; there was no large-scale flight away to other parts of Chicago.[5]

This residential stability of most family heads was not shared by their sons, and in the younger generation the type and size of family in which the sons lived was related to the extent to which they were rooted to the community.

Up to 1880, the residence of sons was remarkably similar to that of their fathers. Since all sons in this trace sample were living in the residential household of their fathers in 1880, it can be assumed this earlier identity of residential distribution meant that few sons had broken away from the parental home in the 1870's only to return in 1880; instead, the data seem to indicate that during the 1870's almost all sons were bound to the parental household.

Graph 5 shows what happened to the residence of sons

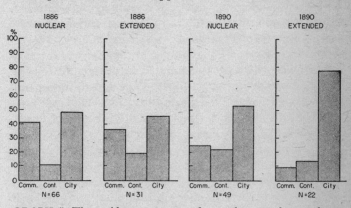

GRAPH 5. The residence patterns of sons from nuclear and extended families; percentages living in Union Park Community, in contiguous areas, and in the city of Chicago

in nuclear and extended families in the 1880's; the patterns of family size were congruent, again, with these results. There was greater rootedness to the community in the 1880's among sons from intensive families than that found in the extended homes. By 1890 nearly half the sons from intensive homes were living in the environs they had grown up in a decade earlier, while more than three quarters of the sons from less intense homes had moved to other parts of the city.

By 1890, there was an 11 percent difference between the heads and sons of nuclear families in their residence concentration in Union Park, a 3 percent difference in concentration in contiguous areas to Union Park, and a 15 percent difference in their concentration in the rest of Chicago. In the extended family, on the other hand, there was a 36 percent difference in concentration in Union Park, a 6 percent difference in concentration in contiguous areas, and a 42 percent difference in concentration in other parts of Chicago. Thus there was an enormous difference between the residence patterns of sons and heads of extended families at the end of this era, contrasted to a much smaller difference between the generations in the nuclear households. Measures of family size revealed the same phenomenon: the process of an intergenerational territorial break was much stronger in the less intense families than in the intensive families.

The intriguing problem is what forces created this situation. These were all elder sons in their middle and late twenties in 1880. Why should those from less intense families have more completely broken away from their parents over the course of a decade? Put another way, why were the sons from intensive families so rooted to the places of their childhood? We have seen that the young men from less intense families were achieving more coherently upward mobility in work during this decade than young men from the dominant family group. The question naturally occurs as to whether the differences in job mobility and rootedness to the community were somehow related.

These problems can have a solution, a solution not through statistics but rather through an effort to imagine what kind of family experience could lead to such processes of social mobility in intensive, isolated homes.

10

THE EVOLUTION OF FAMILY INTENSITY

"In her original attributes, then, the American woman was a fitting and heroic companion to the post-revolutionary man, who was possessed with the idea of freedom from any man's autocracy and haunted by the fear that the nostalgia for some homeland and the surrender to some kin could ever make him give in to political slavery. Mother became 'Mom' only when Father became 'Pop' under the impact of the identical historical discontinuities. For, if you come down to it, Momism is only misplaced paternalism. American mothers stepped into the role of the grandfathers as the fathers abdicated their dominant place in the family, in the field of education, and in cultural life." [1]

What are these "identical historical discontinuities" Erikson speaks of, by which American fathers are said to have lost their authority and their dominance as fathers? In this question about America's family culture there lies the clue to the experience of Union Park fathers and their sons at home and at work.

From the little known of family life in American history, it seems unlikely these historical discontinuities would have come to fruition in the days of the early Republic, in the first few decades of the nineteenth century.

184

Tocqueville, for instance, presents a striking description of the family in 1829–1830. In contrast to the aristocratic mold of the past, where the father was not only "the author and the support of his family, but . . . also its constituted ruler," Tocqueville believed the condition of families in a new country like the United States, "where the government picks out every individual singly from the mass to make him subservient to the general laws of the community, no such intermediate person is required; a father is there, in the eye of the law, only as a member of the community, older and richer than his sons." Thus, given the authoritarian nature of family roles in aristocratic society, Tocqueville concluded that in America the family "in the Roman and aristocratic signification of the word, does not exist." [2] The American father was an absolute ruler only during the period of the child's helplessness.

But this equality of condition did not mean, Tocqueville said, that the father had lost his authority and power. Authority was reconstituted on emotional and experiential bases, rather than on the dictates of law. "In a democratic family the father exercises no other power than that which is granted to the affection and the experience of age; his orders would perhaps be disobeyed, but his advice is for the most part authoritative. Though he is not hedged in with ceremonial respect, his sons at least accost him with confidence; they have no settled form of addressing him, but they speak to him constantly and are ready to consult him every day. The master and the constituted ruler have vanished; the father remains." [3]

Bernard Wishy's research on parents and children of this era bears out Tocqueville's point. In the years before the 1830's, fathers were, he writes, strong-willed companions to their children. Advice, rather than coercion, was the tie between the generations.[4]

This relation of a father to his offspring is not surprising, given the personal and communal looseness of American society before the Civil War. The United States in these early Republic years was an inchoate but energetic society, the people "restless unto death" in Tocqueville's words; no communal institution, as Bernard Bailyn has shown, was stable or strong enough to restrain a son, were his father foolish enough to try making the young man conform to the law or to organized social groups like the churches. Yet the father as a strong *man* existed, Tocqueville says, and this should not be surprising either, for there was no reason for a father to be any less restless, less constant in his search for a different life, than his sons.

This applied particularly to the "Yankees," the men who were fathers to most of the fathers in Union Park. Such perceptive studies as Stanley Elkins' on Negro slavery show the possible reality of stereotypes of a people, pictures one would perhaps be inclined to set aside as "prejudice." Like the stereotype of the Negro slave, the image of the shrewd and avaricious Yankee was too prevalent during the early decades of the nineteenth century to be dismissed as unreal. In the sensitive portrait William R. Taylor paints in *Cavalier and Yankee,* the Yankee was seen by others outside the culture as involved in "crass commercial dealings, shrewd bargaining and even a hint of sharp practices . . . The word Yankee by 1815 clearly invoked for Englishmen the image of a society of monotonous uniformity composed of uncouth and curious rustics whose energies were exclusively given over to pursuit of the main chance." [5] This image of the Yankee, Taylor said, was something the Americans troubled enough to flee abroad saw in themselves as well. A politer name for this grasping was "individualism," though, as Yehoshua Arieli has pointed out, self-seeking individualism was a far different phenomenon from the psychological and aesthetic notions embodied in the Romantics' term "individuality." [6]

Given the reports of Tocqueville and Wishy, and the particular fitness of the Yankee's dynamism for the role of both father and son in Tocqueville's description, it seems unlikely that in the decades of the early Republic American men were passive, silent members of the family. If the change occurred, and spawned in the family a "Mom" whose role dominated, the historical moment must have been later.

Did such a shift occur, then? Students of the American family like Bernard Wishy think that it did, that this shift crystallized finally in the post–Civil War generation. Yet Wishy has no real explanation as to why the change took place. In the lives of the Union Park people, the reason for and the process of this father weakness comes clear, as a part of a larger influence of the growing new city on these families who inhabited it. The data on Union Park, I believe, suggest how as the intensive family came to serve as the main primary-group defense against the new energies of an industrial city, the position of the father in the urban family weakened. The following pages explore how the Union Park father might have lost his acquisitive energy, and thereby part of his manhood in this culture, out of fearful withdrawal into the shelter of his family. This change in fatherhood was the sad, and certainly unintended, consequence of a stance the middle class families of Union Park assumed toward an era of rapid social change in their city.

The documentary history of Union Park suggested two contrasting accounts of the role of men in families; interestingly, neither of these fits Tocqueville's description of vigorous families. H. C. Chatfield-Taylor's father was an autocrat and, unlike the "egalitarians" Tocqueville described, an aristocrat. Chatfield-Taylor's father ruled his home with the iron hand of religion, and asceticism in the family was the condition to which he directed his strength, just as it was a sign of his own virtue. The family men depicted by F. W. Wilkie, chronicler of Union Park a generation later, when it was dominated by the middle classes, appeared "docile and retiring," while their wives were "strong-willed" and "active." These Union Park family women and men were, in other words, the kind of people who figure in Erikson's account of families where Mom holds the reins of power and the children feel that the father somehow does not matter. The independent, restless father of Tocqueville's day was not found among these sedate burghers and their strong-willed wives.[7]

For this particular community, then, the result of some "historical discontinuities" produced signs of the phenomenon Erikson, or in another context, Kenneth Keniston, have so sensitively described. From the structure of these families during one year and their patterns of mobility over time, it is possible to see what groups this shift in the family affected, and, why Erikson's historical discontinuities came to occur.

Family Cycles: The Stages of Interaction between the Family and the City

We have seen that small families and nuclear families in Union Park tended to have very similar characteristics of employment among fathers and sons, and similar patterns of residence. Conditions of family life associated with a less intensive or sheltered household in 1880, such as extended kin forms or large families, showed over the course of twenty years patterns also working in tandem, and in an opposite direction from that of the intensive family forms.

The models of intensive family life that follow attempt to portray the combined effect of forces like small size, nuclear form, or intensive life-stage patterns, on the human beings behind the statistical structures. These models are "ideal-typical" pictures, in that they seek to uncover the logical structure behind the convergent forces of family intensiveness. For many families, obviously, forces of small size and nuclear form and an intensive life-stage pattern did not all converge at the same time and in the same way. Like any model, the cycle of intensive family life presented here describes a polar condition, in which individual people or families were enmeshed to varying degrees.

The model of historical development explored is termed a "family cycle"; it indicates not how the experience of an original generation of urbanites was reduplicated in the lives of their progeny, but rather how the effects of this experience were transmitted to the sons, as a problem that had to be dealt with under a new set of historical circumstances.

The history of Union Park families was actually that of two different concurrent family cycles, one for the dominant group of intensive families, and a contrasting one for the minority of less intensive families. The divide between these two cycles helps explain how the family, and the father's role in the family, in the dominant family group, came to differ from the situation prevailing in the early Republic. It also suggests how, for a smaller number of families, the family continued to function in the industrial city as it had in earlier generations. This small group of families possessed, in other words, both a continuity with the past and a greater effectiveness in coping with the

Two Family Cycles

A. The Dominant Cycle

Outside the Family   *Within the Family*

I. Migration to the city: sense of dislocation and "lostness."

II. Drawing together of intensive families as havens of comfort and security.

late 1860's 1870's

III. Stasis or decline in work patterns of fathers in the labor force; emphasis on maintaining what one has securely.

IV. Fathers present defensive picture of urban world to sons; growing sense of distance in the family in relations between fathers and sons who are beginning to work.

V. Sons begin to become occupationally mobile in unsteady and patternless fashion; confusion related to their relative lack of innovation in where they live in the city; cannot break away from the haunts of their youth.

1880's

VI. Sons cease looking to father for guidance in outer world; father becomes more and more passive in the role relationship of family; sons begin to focus on mother as the dominant parent.

VII

1890's 1900's

Combination of instability in work and apathetic response to concrete events in community create a social bleakness for the sons, a condition of social isolation and aimlessness that makes them weak in the urban world. This anomie becomes then the means by which their own sons will perceive them in the future as "absent," as weak guides to the conduct of life.

B. The Minority Cycle

Outside the Family   *Within the Family*

I. Migration to the city: sense of dislocation.

II. Presence of working collateral kin or of large numbers of family of all ages, makes family unit as a whole more work oriented; family unit has difficulty acting as a shelter from the world. Family energies partly turned toward the world at large.

late 1860's 1870's

III. Mobile work patterns among adults; trend of the mobility is generally upward to white collar status; possibly a coherent wave pattern of upward movement in the white collar classes.

IV. Fathers have an ego-integration in their work that can be communicated in rearing the sons. A defensive restrictive world view is not necessary for them, since they are succeeding under dynamic economic conditions.

V. Sons become occupationally mobile in steady and patterned fashion, generally upward; freedom of residential location, and a greater intergenerational break.

1880's

VI. Possible for sons to look to parents for guidance in the outer world, since parents have also had the experience of mobility; father does therefore "count" in the experiences of the sons' lives.

VII

1890's 1900's

An emotional rapport between the generations, like the earlier process noticed by Tocqueville; the basis of the bond is a common experience of change and movement, so that the residential split between generations ultimately severs the physical ties between generations, though the strength and dignity of the parents is maintained. This is the process of healthy intergenerational break.

emerging urban society than did the family form that existed in Union Park as a prevailing response to the industrial city. The accompanying chart presents a schematic outline of the differences in these two family cycles.

The Dominant Family Cycle

Stage One: Migration to the city creating a sense of dislocation. In America, the prevailing images of the industrial city of a century ago were images of a terrifying, evil, unstable place and images of an exciting, convoluted habitat, one to be explored in all its diversity.[8] To those who migrated to these cities, the images of terror may well have been felt more keenly once the migrants had actually arrived. Frank Lloyd Wright's *Autobiography*, for instance, recounted the dread of a young man when in 1887, at age eighteen, he moved from a small town in Wisconsin to Chicago.

Wright remembered the enormous crowds "intent on seeing nothing." He felt lost amid all these people, as if he were really helpless. In the mass of city people downtown, he was, he imagined at the time, stranded without any potential friends or people who would assist him: "there was only the brutal, hurrying crowd" protecting themselves by ignoring him.[9]

Such images were familiar ones for Chicago; they run through Dreiser's *Sister Carrie*, or the early writings of Sherwood Anderson. In Wright's case, the sense of terror finally won out over the excitement; he felt he had to establish some bulwark against this world, some region that was protective and safe. The way in which he found safety is one many young men newly come to Union Park also found: marriage. Wright took as a wife one of the first girls he ever dated, and he set to work on establishing himself solidily in a career. He did no wandering as a young man, had no "psycho-social moratorium" where he floated free for a few years as a bohemian; as soon as possible, he made things secure for himself, by marrying and founding a family, and by beginning immediately the diligent pursuit of his work.

This marriage was a disaster for him later in his life, when Wright came to recognize it to be born out of fear, and the need to be immediately secure. But the pattern of Wright's migration provides a clue to what happened to many of the people of Union Park; his founding of a family, as a bulwark against the new and alien social life in the city, was something shared by the dominant group of Union Park family men.

Stage Two: The drawing together of families. One striking feature of the process of founding a family in Union Park was the short space of time between breaking away from home and marriage. The nature of the intergenerational break, for the majority, did not lead a young man to experiment in living alone for a while, but rather, parallel to Wright's experience, the break was soon succeeded by a re-establishment of the same conjugal family pattern.

Instead of breaking down under urban conditions, family life showed itself to be tenaciously strong, so that the young repeated as soon as they could the domestic situation of their elders. There was in addition little tendency for fathers and married sons or daughters to live together, in a two-generation extended family; thus there was across the generations of this community an emphasis on the privacy as well as the primacy of the intensive family condition.

The data from both directory trace and the 1880 Census indicate intensive family life was not produced or determined economically as a result of interaction with the changing work force. The most plausible explanation for the strength of such families seems to me rather to be in terms of how people moving to a city would have perceived their society: the intensive family was strong because it was a means of quelling the fear and uncertainty men experienced in these new urban places. What, then, would have to be the elements of an intensive family that could be used as "weapons of defense" against the city?

In Chatfield-Taylor's reminiscence of his youth in the 1860's, he recalled that the family in church on Sunday was not the sole social activity of the day. "Young sports," aristocratic gentlemen of more hedonistic tastes, paraded their horses and carriages in front of church, to the scandalized tongue-clucking of those inside. One point of this story is that no one in the church left his pew after the service to join these impious ones because everybody else in the family would have known; we can well imagine the thunder the father of young Chatfield-Taylor would have loosed on the boy if after church he went to talk to friends who were "young sports" or take a ride in a fashionable lady's carriage.

Now imagine, at a point in time after the Civil War, a family where the father's righteous morality did not serve him as a sign of his elite status, as it did for Chatfield-Taylor's father; here the family would be middle class, and not so prominent in community life. Still, in an intensive family such as this, everyone could know what everyone else was doing. The family may have been private vis-à-vis its relations with the outside world, but it was extremely unprivate as regards the knowledge the family members could have of each other's doings. One thinks of the Bennet sisters in *Pride and Prejudice,* and their constant probing into the details of each other's lives; such a situation would be even greater in families living not in rural country houses, nor in city houses for that matter, but in apartment boardinghouses such as Carrie Meeber in Dreiser's *Sister Carrie* lived in. (This is, it should be recalled, the era when the apartment house came into its own as a dwelling place for urban families.[10])

Such an absence of internal privacy between members of the family meant that the family members did have, of necessity, absolute face-to-face relations with each other; the fragmentation and sense of disjointed conglomeration of many private worlds, experienced outside in the city, was replaced by an overwhelming sense of intimacy within the house. The family group was the only coherent primary association into which men of Union Park could retreat. In this way, someone uneasy in the large world found in the home a situation of the most direct and unimpeded contact with other people. This is how the intensive family, especially that of small size, could have given its members a sense of intimacy and direct personal contacts within the family circle, while at the same time it became a unit totally unlike the diverse worlds of experience that lay outside the home.

So the first condition of the intensive family in Union Park as a bulwark against the industrial city lay in the conditions of privacy vis-à-vis the outer world and the non-private intimacy within the family itself. But the primacy of the family was reinforced in another way as well.

It appears that the addition of children to the family was regular and highly controlled, since in 1880 the families in general tended to have small numbers of progeny. Given the absence of good birth control technology and general lack of desire to use what mechanical means were available, a rigid self-discipline between the conjugal pair accounted for this limitation, so that abstinence regulated the family's size.

It is a commonplace in the study of "primitive" social groups that objects of the greatest fear are also endowed with the greatest sanctity; the anxieties of fearing something are in part sublimated by endowing the object itself with the highest and most awesome qualities. This idea has been given technical description by such theorists as L. Festinger, in his concept of "cognitive dissonance." Something similar, it appears, occurred among the urban families of Union Park. Here, sex and pregnancy were anxious to a degree difficult today to imagine; the body's natural processes were engaged in continual warfare with the morals of society and the economics of family life. In this situation it would be only natural that the conjugal family assumed a kind of haloed importance in men's lives, as a means of transforming some of the guilt and uneasiness men and women felt into more positive expressions of mutuality. The sanctity of the family, so common, so insistent an image of the nineteenth century, could have been an ideal that alleviated in part the real suffering these people felt in conducting married life according to the dictates and values of their time; by making the family unit sacred, its trials were justified.[11]

In such a situation, where the family was intense, where the members of the family had little privacy from each other, and where the strains of a man and a woman living together were in part allayed by raising the family idea itself to a position of religious sanctity, it would be natural that though a man's energies were spent at the office or store his allegiances would lie at home. For men confused and scared by the new city, the family offered an intimate world with an internal binding power of its own: both the city and the nature of the family unit would lead men to become absorbed in "home."

In this condition lies the special relevance of family size

to the dominant family cycle, for this pattern of withdrawal would have been stronger, the fewer the individuals that had to be knit into the family frame. The sociological commonplace that smaller families are more intense emotionally than larger, looser ones thus had a historical dimension: when the family itself served as a refuge from the city at large, rather than a means of adaptation to it, the smaller family lent itself easily to an internal intensity, a lack of emotional privacy within the house.

If this portrait approximates the dominant experience of Union Park families, then it is also reasonable to suppose men tried to survive in the city by holding on to what they did in work — and concentrated their involvement and emotional capacities in the intimate area of wife and child. In this way, the desire to be mobile would be blunted; a man would hope to hold on in the chaos of the city, and develop himself within the circle of people he loved and who loved him.

Stage Three: The impact of intense family life. The idea just advanced runs counter to a common stereotype, that of the father working as hard as he can at the office, making and risking as much as he can, in order to better the lives of his wife and children. The stereotype has several flaws in it; logically, a man who is engrossed in his family is going to be very cautious about risking his job or his capital. Such risk was in fact a fearful image to the bourgeoisie of the nineteenth century. The business failures that occurred in novels like *Vanity Fair* or *The House of Mirth* were not the result of steady decline, but of some speculative investment that suddenly went bad: chance was the road to ruin.

The stereotype of the entrepreneurial father also has a flaw in terms of the ideologies of mobility that existed at the time. In his excellent study of the ideologies of upward mobility, *Apostles of the Self-made Man*, John Cawelti has shown the images of mobility current at this time to be more a movement from lower class to prosperous middle class than from poverty to the wealth of someone like Andrew Carnegie. The ideal was for a man to become bourgeois; the dream of endless riches, such as one finds in the "Acres of Diamonds" speech, was not the dominant voice in this conception of achieving the good life. The dominant theme was rather to be found in the Horatio Alger stories, where the boy made it up out of poverty as a youth through some sudden good fortune, and then stayed comfortably and stably middle class during his own adulthood.[12]

The third flaw in the concept of the urban middle class father as a raw, mobile entrepreneur on the model of Tocqueville's restless Americans can be demonstrated by the concrete statistics of this study. There was, quite simply, an absence of such a process for the fathers of the dominant family form in Union Park. The strength of family life, rather than the pursuit of upward mobility in the big city, seems to have been an alternative path of concern for such men. That the desire to rise was present cannot, of course, be denied. But the "failure" of these fathers to be mobile to the extent fathers from a different family configuration were may indicate that the intensive family was chosen as a place of refuge and center of life, not merely forced upon these men by circumstances.[13] It was in the results of such a combination of choice and circumstance that these intensive-family fathers encountered a domestic tragedy: the product of their absorption in the family made fathers seem weak in the eyes of their sons.

The tracing of intensive-family fathers revealed their occupational distribution to have been fairly static across a long period of time. This does not mean that there was no movement of individuals among occupational types; indeed, the data on direct occupational change suggest that the intensive family had an instability at the highest level of work and in the lower white collar groups. But the family heads of this dominant kinship system taken as a group showed little change over the course of time. This raises a methodological problem, familiar since Durkheim made analyses of group movement on similar grounds: how can one infer from the group pattern the experience of the specific human beings who composed the group?

The answer to this problem is, I believe, one of common sense. It would be difficult to explain how, over the course of eighteen years, during the most sweeping changes in the nature of work in Chicago, the group of intensive-family leaders had a work pattern that remained stable, yet somehow the individuals in it were so mobile that no significant generalizations can be made about the whole. It is a more direct proposition, as argued here, to say that the general pattern of occupational "freeze" did indicate the experience of large numbers of individual men. Direct measures of occupational change, which were after all restricted to a much smaller sample, showed that within this general pattern of freeze some people were experiencing mobility, though of a disadvantageous sort when compared to the mobility of the minority group of extensive-family leaders. Thus there existed a gross pattern of stability among the generations of intensive-family fathers, with some mobile patterns usually unfavorable to the father's status.

How did this job freeze, in the midst of a society these men found threatening, affect the way they raised their children? How did it affect the sense of being a parent in a family group now a weapon of defense against, and refuge from, the city?

Stage Four: Preparing the children for the city. One

piece of modern research offers a clue. In the work of David Aberle and Kaspar Naegele on "Middle-Class Fathers' Occupational Role and Attitudes toward Children," it was found that the fathers themselves perceive, at first, no relationship between their job situation and their behavior at home. Aberle and Naegele cite two reasons for this feeling: first, that the "impersonality" of bureaucratic selection requires a divide between the life of worker and father; second, that competitive drives innate to work are not thought to be appropriate to home. But Aberle and Naegele find a tendency among the fathers to look in their sons for exactly those qualities that will make the sons function successfully in their work: competitiveness, aggressiveness, and so forth. Thus, the sons' present behavior is being constantly scrutinized for its worth in the future, as a tool for the son's occupational future, rather than for its worth in the present family context. Although the fathers do not see themselves as teaching their sons the arts of aggression, they expect the sons, somehow, to generate a competitive desire to get ahead.[14]

Let us try to imagine this situation in an earlier historical context, at a seminal point of growth of an industrial city. The middle class fathers of Union Park were defensive rather than responsive to the work world growing in Chicago at this time; the family was an intensive, sanctified institution in the midst of the immense, impersonal city developing. In this context, there might have been an even more marked gulf between family and work situation than what Aberle and Naegele describe for our own time. At this earlier point, the fathers were not themselves aggressive, to judge from available evidence, but defensive, and the family would have been the weapon they used for defense. The result should have been a tremendous confusion in the "signals" the fathers passed down to their sons, much greater, again, than the discontinuity Aberle and Naegele find in the middle class families of our own day. For while the fathers would have hoped for the success of their sons in the world, there would also be great anxiety about what they were preparing the young for. This anxiety was not the product of some self-conscious and sophisticated alienation, but arose out of the fact that the fathers were going nowhere themselves; they had not the gift of their own experience, in coping with something new, raw, chaotic, and vigorous, to pass on to their sons, no experience of "how I met this challenge" to give to their sons as a model.

Fathers with such work experience in their own lives must have made warnings to their sons a dominant theme of preparation for the work the sons would perform, warnings of the dangers of the industrial world, the pitfalls of being impetuous, the unknown disasters that could come so unexpectedly to the individual worker. The dominant mode of training would have then been in the arts of caution and restraint, in the midst of an economic order which was anything but cautious, anything but orderly and restrained. As part of the family, an institution that served the fathers themselves as refuge, the fathers would have seen themselves in relation to their sons as a shield against all that lay outside the home.

This capacity to act as a shield would well have suited certain structural properties of the intensive family, properties discernible in the census materials of 1880. For, in most Union Park families, there was only one worker in the house, the father; working wives were a rare phenomenon even in the poorer classes. Here the intensiveness of the home was shaped by family form; the single adult worker was a condition of nuclear families much more than of extended families, for in the extended families collateral kin were employed, and so the adult generation had more than one kin member engaged in the economic activities of the city. Thus the nuclear-family father could have exercised a clear and unchallenged role as the mediator between the home and the city, could have singly interpreted the happenings of their society to those in the family shelter.

Yet as the young men in nuclear families grew up, they could not have helped but observe, as did young Chatfield-Taylor, the differences between home and the society around it. A trip downtown to go shopping, the walk to and from school, perhaps an occasional, unauthorized sortie with some friends into the forbidden reaches of the city, all these could have awakened in a young man that alternative image of the city as an exciting, exotic place to be explored. But most of of all, the Union Park data showed, sons from intensive families began to experience something unlike the world view of their fathers when they, the sons, began their own adult lives.

Stage Five: Mobile sons. Over the course of fourteen years, these young men experienced occupational change, not stability. The sons from intensive homes had therefore an occupational experience unlike that of their fathers, for they were dynamic in their work patterns, and this dynamism involved significant drops in status as well as gains upward. Moreover, in the dominant family group, sons were not able to make significant territorial breaks from their parents to the same degree found in the less intense family form; these young men were rooted to Union Park and its surroundings.

Thus, the majority of these young people experienced at the same time an unstable pattern of work and confinement to the homes of their childhood or adolescence. Why the sons stayed in their youthful surroundings is a speculative problem difficult to resolve. Perhaps the best explanation would be that they were unwillingly caught up in the dynamism of the world of work because they were so young; it was difficult for them, as work groups, to protect positions an older generation could guard by virtue of experience or seniority. The desire to remain in the world they knew — even during its years of declining respectability — was an expression of an inner need for stability, of a desire for a territory that was theirs.

The importance of this situation is in what it meant for the way the sons of intensive families viewed their past and those who constituted their past, namely their parents. It is here we find the material to explain Erikson's observation that, in retrospect, many bourgeois American fathers seem not to "count" in the eyes of their sons.

Stage Six: The relations of fathers and sons, of fathers and mothers. What would a son who was experiencing fluctuations in his work, while remaining in or near the community of his parents, have felt about the "authoritative advice" Tocqueville pictured from father to son in a previous generation? The available evidence showed Union Park fathers to be static in the city work forum, and to be, plausibly, defensive about their work. Sons who were then experiencing instability would not be able to turn to their fathers and the experiences of their fathers as models or guides for what they should do in their own situation. The experience of the younger generation was discontinuous with the experience of the older; a condition of instability succeeded a condition of stability. The fathers' counsel would be one of caution, telling the sons to avoid instability, but the sons were unstable, perhaps against their will. The advice they could use would logically be from someone who had harnessed the dynamism of the urban work structure successfully, but such fathers were not among the majority in Union Park, but among the small minority of heads of less intense families.

This view challenges the theory of S. N. Eisenstadt, in his monumental work on age groupings, *From Generation to Generation,* that upward mobility across generations is achieved by breaks between the values of the generations, even though a common, general outlook and mutuality is maintained between fathers and sons. Eisenstadt believes that "The modern father in urban Europe and America does not usually behave similarly at home with his family group and in his place of work. And if his child is to achieve occupational status of some sort he must learn to behave differently than he does with regard to his father within the scope of their family life, although his general orientation to the occupational field is derived from identification with the father." [15] Eisenstadt's theory is a good one, for a fairly stable historical situation. But in times of great and rapid change, the emotional need for guidance extends beyond a shared "general orientation" of beliefs; the young need to learn from the old what they should do, specifically, to cope with the society that is in flux around them. Were Eisenstadt's theory generally valid, the sons of intense families should have performed more satisfactorily than the sons of less intense families, since the fathers from intensive families provided what Eisenstadt calls a "negative model" against which sons could rebel and define new values of their own.

On the contrary, "the historical discontinuities" by which the father ceased to be a strong member of the family in the eyes of his sons came about in this way: the father's failure to be dynamic in the world ultimately made him fail as a father, for he had no real gift of experience to give to his sons who were ineluctably caught outside the home in forces they could not control. The passivity and "docileness" of these fathers stood out at the time so that even a gross intelligence like Wilkie's singled it out as a peculiar trait of this middle class community. The static position of these fathers in the midst of a revolution in the urban economy was the play of social forces that brought this condition of family character about.

The passivity that Wilkie and Dreiser noted in these homes concerned the relations of fathers to their wives rather than to their children. Yet the origin of this passivity in the family would have been the same in both cases; the man as a creature with identities and strengths outside the circle of home life would have been eclipsed, so that within the home he had little uniquely his own as a man to give. The statistics showed his immobility in work, his half failure in a world where movement and acquisition were the hallmarks of success. Whether the concentration on home life was a result or a cause of this half failure, the reverberations in the home finally bore the stamp of a hard irony, for the man was little more the master here than in the outer world. He had no exploits, no claims of personal power, and so no independence of his own.

Thus when Wilkie remarked that the women of Union Park seemed constantly to be pushing the men to be more successful and that the men needed to be pushed because they were shy and retiring, he had grasped in a crude way the product of complex patterns of work and family structure that defined the role of Union Park men to both their wives and their offspring. The sons of course could not try to push their fathers as the wives could. In the circumstances of change in which these urbanites lived, the sons logically would have wanted more to be led than to lead.

This conclusion about feeling from known behavior accords not only with the observations of contemporaries, but with the character of the changes occurring in Union

Park as people passed from the family of orientation to the family of procreation. The data from 1880 revealed that large numbers of young men remained in their parents' home throughout their twenties and early thirties. This phenomenon is explicable given the fact, revealed in the tracing, that their careers outside the home were unstable. To live on one's own meant one had to be able to establish a condition of economic security. Similarly, marriages would not be undertaken until the man had established this security to the woman's satisfaction. Being economically secure was the accomplishment that gave a young man the right to live a full and independent life; yet the goal was a difficult one, for in the dominant families instability was his lot, and there was nothing in the experience of his parents to draw on.

If the process of breaking away from home was difficult, and extended over a great length of time, the tension in staying there must have been just as great. To the young man whose fortunes in the city were fluctuating, the parental advice of caution and stability surely was aggravating and unreal, when the young man himself had not enough experience or resources to be able to be stable, in control of his own fate. The pattern of waiting to marry until one was established in the work world compounded the young man's instability with a graver problem, whether he would ever earn the privilege to have full sexual relations with a woman and generate children of his own. Thus was the path of movement for the young burdened with a great deal of tension and, probably, a great deal of pain.

For these middle class families of Chicago, the sense of "father absence" in the minds of the sons Erikson speaks of should be broadened to include what Robert J. Lifton has termed a feeling of "counterfeit-nurturance" among adolescents and young adults.[16] The sons of Union Park, in the dominant family form, had not been prepared for the world, but had grown up in a kinship group resembling more a refugee shelter; yet at a later stage of their own development they had to live in the city, and make something of all its complexities. The preparation for this task lay, it was conceived at the time, with the father, yet his guidance was not in terms of meeting the world, but rather in fleeing from it into the intimacy of the home, while simply staying stable in the broader society. In this way the sons may have felt not only that their fathers were weak but that their "fatherliness," as a guide, a voice of experience and knowledge about what lay outside the home, was counterfeit, not true to the outer world as the sons so painfully experienced it.

The Census shows that the young people in 1880 recapitulated the impulse to tight family life; there were experiments in intermarriage between cultures, but there were no experiments in the process of marriage itself. That was their own slavery to the intensity of family to which they were born. But the slavery had a new dimension.

Stage Seven: The outcome of the family cycle in the next generation. The combination of instability in work and clinging to home makes the lives of these sons seem bleak, and indeed they probably were. It is difficult to think of middle class urbanites as "disadvantaged" or "deprived" in the way poor people in the city were, yet humanly and emotionally, on this account, they were deprived, not prepared to deal with the city as the sons from the minority family group were. One senses intuitively a kind of emotional poverty, a species of the isolation and aimlessness in these lives Durkheim called anomie.

Yet, these sons did not drift alone, but rather could make their own defenses against the outer world, by immediately founding new households once the break from their parents' home was accomplished. It seems logical that the family would be used in this second generation for refuge and shelter as much as was true in the parents' generation. In this way, the "refugee" outlook of the first-generation fathers could pass down to the sons, whose own progeny, when they matured into young adulthood, would sense *their* fathers to be distant from the world, absent and unable to guide action in it, and thus unable to serve as a model.

In this way, a historical discontinuity, developed in the middle class of four generations ago, might have descended into the urban middle class Americans of modern times to shape the lives of people such as those Erikson and Keniston describe.

The Minority Family Cycle

The stages of the minority family cycle, involving "less intensive" families, presented clear contrasts to the dominant mode of family interaction in Union Park. The initial migration to the big city presumably engaged people in the same tremors as those felt in the dominant family form; there is no reason to assume any different reaction to this new and frightening form of social life.

But through the structural formation of their family group, whatever desires they had to use the family as a tool of withdrawal were inhibited. Family form was one inhibitor. In 1880, the extended families were, as a unit, more work-oriented functionally, because more of the adult generation was engaged in the labor force; this in turn was the result of the structural character of the extended families — they were extended by the presence of working collateral kin in the adult generation. Family size also played a role, especially if one of the children was old enough to work. There must have been much more talk between family members, at dinner or on days off, about work; the working members would inevitably have compared their different positions, and probably competition would have arisen, for within the family circle someone else existed to whom one's own work experience could be compared, evaluated, and judged.

Thus it would have been much more difficult to insulate the family circle against the outer world; the structural conditions of the family inevitably brought one's performance in the outer world into the family, and formed a part of the stance that adult family members took toward each other. The practice of not "talking business," of leaving behind the office and what one did there when work was done for the day, would be an unnatural mode for the adult family members, whereas it would be natural when only one member of the family worked, as in most nuclear families. In this way, the minority families built a bridge between the home and the city life outside it.

The result of this situation emerged in the data on how these less intensive family adults performed in their work. In contrast to the heads of intensive families, the less intensive family leaders changed their occupational configuration over the course of time, in a generally upward direction, and with the disappearance of both skilled and unskilled labor from their ranks over the eighteen-year period. Their experience as a class of workers was that of upward mobility.

The reason for this achievement we lay to the fact of their work life being under greater scrutiny at home, often in competition with the work pattern of another adult who, as collateral kin, lived in the family. One's work was not something that could be kept from the family, in the sense that one would be evaluated as a family member apart from it; there were others within the family circle who were also striving outside and who provided a point of reference, or in some cases may have supplemented or helped one's own efforts. In either event, the split between home and work was harder to maintain; the two worlds became interwoven and, for these families in Union Park, the outcome was favorable for the work experience of the family leader.

What was the impact of this presence of work on children being reared in such families? They heard a great deal about work from the perspective of more than one worker's job experience; and the facts of work, the comparisons between the different kinds of jobs, were something they would immediately know through dinner-table discussions or casual talk. If the family adults were engaged in joint business, a similar process of family participation in the work lives of the adults would ensue.

But more than this, the experience of their fathers in the work structure of the city was a successful one on the whole; large numbers of these fathers were moving out of jobs where they used their hands to more administrative and executive positions. What the children heard, the kinds of experience they assimilated, were those of successful adults, not the reflections of fathers who, like those in the contrasting dominant family group, were fairly static in their jobs, in the midst of the unfolding of a new order of enterprise and industry. Their success probably made such fathers less defensive about their work experiences, permitted them wholeheartedly to encourage in their sons those arts of aggressiveness and initiative which they themselves evidently possessed.

Again, we can only guess that this process occurred by judging its fruits, the capacities of the sons of these families to achieve something in their own work. In contrast to the sons from the dominant family mode, the sons from less intensive families were coherently upwardly mobile. Theirs was a greater achievement of middle class status over the course of time, and a greater aggregate concentration in the upper levels of the middle classes than their intensive-family counterparts; this upward mobility was different in form from that of their fathers, but upward mobility still.

Thus it was possible for the minority of sons to look to their fathers for guidance and advice, to treat the father as a strong member of the family, because he *was* strong; he had adapted to the world in a way in which they themselves were moving. In contrast to the intergenerational situation in the dominant family group, the father here counted not only because he himself had resources to harness change for his own and his family's betterment, but because his experience was relevant to that of his sons.

Since the sons of less intensive families started off with roughly the same distribution in the labor force as intensive-family sons, and then achieved more over the course of time, some part of their gain must be attributable to the circumstances of their upbringing; it cannot be traced to a specially favored start economically at the beginning of their careers. Were the differences resolved into simple economics — so that the sons of less intensive families were said to achieve more because their families, having achieved more, could give them more help and support in starting out — the psychological condition would of course remain the same: the father stood as a source of strength to the sons, as someone who was to be counted on and respected. But because of the equality in starting positions between sons of dominant and minority family types, a mechanistic model along these simple economic lines does violence to the data: if it were *only* a question of money, surely the occupational configurations between sons in the two family forms would show some marked differences at the beginning of work. The upbringing of the child, his day-by-day initiation to the work world in a nonsheltered family, must have played some additional role; the outcome of this process of extensive family development would be, then, a condition of respect between two generations of dynamic workers.

This condition of emotional rapport between the generations gave a special cast to the residential breaks that occurred in this extended-family form. These sons were much more mobile out of the Union Park area and its environs than sons from the dominant homes; especially at the end of the era, these extended-family sons tended to move away whereas their fathers responded by sticking out the community's decline.

The character of a residential break between generations surely was different in homes where the family members in both generations were dynamic individuals than in homes where residential stability mirrored a static work response to changing work conditions in the city. The residential split would not be laden with that sense of rejection of the older generation one might ordinarily ascribe to it, for the expectation in these extended families was exactly one of change and movement. It was a process both generations had experienced and dealt with in a manner advantageous to themselves. There was no deep challenge to the parents when the sons moved out, or rather, perhaps the pain of the break between generations was not clouded over with that sense of dependency on the young, the leaning on them, in families where the elders had failed to create something satisfying and autonomous of their own. In this way, the break between generations in the extended family, rapid as it was, was a sign of a healthy form of intergenerational movement and not an indicator of pathology. Indeed, the greater rootedness of the dominant family sons to the places of their youth may be a sign of that disengagement from society, that anomie, that Durkheim found to be the hidden pathology of the industrial culture of this time.

The extended family was in this way historically continuous, not discontinuous, with the families Tocqueville saw in an earlier generation. Though the extended-family fathers felt a bond to Union Park and its environs during a time of trouble, the residence patterns indicate this concern was not communicated to their sons in any command form that prohibited the sons from following a movement plan of their own. More important, in the extended family, both generations were occupationally dynamic and explorative of possibilities in the new work structures of the city; there was a continuity of generations, and thus a reason why the sons would turn to their fathers for advice about the problems the sons encountered in the work world.

Considered from a demographic viewpoint, this kinship form was a small minority of an urban population, even though this historically continuous form had superior functional capacities in a new social environment, that of the large city. A discontinuity in the city was created, not through the evolution of a new family form, for the work of John Demos, Phillip Greven, and Peter Laslett has established the prior existence of nonmetropolitan nuclear families, but through some special *metropolitan* use the dominant family served, a use that did not involve functional responsiveness to the industrial structures of the new city.

The Meaning of the Family Cycles:
A Failure in American Pluralism

This contrast between the dominant and the minority family cycles shows the questions of Union Park's history to have been all questions about one whole. The character of the fathers in these homes, so different from that of the upper class era before the Civil War, was a product of the same family process that created the privacy and secluded intensity for which these middle class families were re-marked at the time. Yet the privacy and seclusion, whether a willful imposition of order against the disorder of indus-trial Chicago or an involuntary recoil, ended in cutting off fathers from those they had brought to maturity, so that the fathers appeared weak, the mothers strong, and the quality of the upbringing, in a modern phrase, "counter-feit." To account for the passivity of these men in their families is then to account for a whole process of family development, extending across the generations: the posi-tion of the father, the character of the home, and the quality of training of the young, all were part of a larger dialogue, through work, between the dominant order of primary-group life and the city, its enormity and its confu-sions.

The study of the Union Park families — whose terms of analysis derive from the almost global theories of Parsons and Ariès, and whose results tend to affirm the validity of Ariès idea against that of Parsons — is an urban study. The families of Union Park were more than "an element" of the massive sweep of bureaucratization or rationaliza-tion, as Parsons would have it; they were men engaged in a dialogue with city life at a particular time and place, and the result of this dialogue was a tragedy all its own. The

214

retreat into the family ended by destroying the bonds of family across the generations so that men who sought safety in the home became finally passive and weak within its borders. This urban process is what brought these particular people under the general rubric of family intensity set out by Ariès.

The pluralism of American life has been, in the view of many observers, the most striking aspect of the society, and the historical condition passed most stably from one generation to the next. Broadly, this pluralism has been taken as the outcome of the break from feudal society entailed in American development; in place of a hierarchic community, ideally bound together so that the parts serve to articulate a common whole, the American community from the time of the Revolution and early Republic has been held to be a world in which the parts, and the individuals who compose the parts, have maintained lives of their own. Instead of common or unified community life, Americans have across time experienced a series of different communities of interest, a plethora of social roles that do not form a harmonious unit but rather a loosely knit, often conflicting, set or groups of social ideals. Such pluralism, argues Oscar Handlin, forms the basis for a distinctive pattern of liberty in the United States, a liberty gained at the expense of coherence and communal purity.[17]

Nowhere should such pluralism have been more deep-rooted than in the industrial cities that grew up in America at the end of the nineteenth century. Older towns were suddenly inundated with massive numbers of people from the farms and villages of the country; new and enormous cities, such as Chicago, sprung up in the space of decades, and after 1890, wave upon wave of foreign peasants and petit bourgeois swelled the urban populace. There was little in the tradition or structure of these cities to bind the generations of newcomers together, no central form of control nor central agency of allegiance to make all these diverse elements one whole.

This appearance of pluralism in the American city was, indeed, the character of its life singled out for analysis in the work of the first American urban sociologists — Robert Park, Louis Wirth, and others in the "Chicago School," sociologists at the University of Chicago in the 1920's and 1930's. For Park, the industrial city was a mass of separate worlds in which the individual participated; for Wirth the process of urbanization was, psychologically, a process by which the individual himself became pluralistic in his values and capacities for action. This "segmentation," as Wirth called it, was a taking of the diversities in the milieu around the individual into the individual himself, so that his identity became a function of all the separate, and often irreconcilable, activities and interests into which he was thrust in the city; for Wirth, the city was the greatest destroyer of the purity of self, the condition of society that made it almost impossible for an individual man to act and believe as a single and unified being.[18]

These descriptions of American pluralism, and its intensification under modern urban conditions, diverge sharply from the experience of families in Union Park, for the import of the dominant family cycle was precisely a flight from urban pluralism, pluralism that produced disorder, chaos, or a sense of being lost. It is not that these descriptions of pluralism are incorrect, but rather that they describe a potential for social life that the majority of the Union Park fathers and sons did not seize. These good family men, a first generation of the industrial city's middle class, did not take the plurality of urban society into their own lives, but rather sought to maintain the singleness and purity of their emotional lives in the sanctity of the home. This defense against emotional plurality in themselves, this unwillingness to give themselves up to the disunity of the city, but a desire rather to preserve a region of intimate life which in its privacy was sheltering and intense, led the fathers to disaster in the family itself. The father in the eyes of his offspring became a weakling who did not count, who failed to prepare the sons for their own tasks in the world. This failure in turn led the young people to reestablish, out of their anomie, a refuge for themselves in families of their own and so perhaps perpetuate the cycle of "counterfeit-nurturance" of the young for social life.

Family life that responded to the dynamic pluralism of the city did not disappear in Union Park, but the history of less intensive families, so much of a piece with the family development Tocqueville saw in the early years of the Republic, was that of a minority, and arose out of the fortuitous structure of the family group. But for the majority of families, there was a failure in the first generation of middle class urbanites to establish a condition of pluralism that would be meaningful and productive for themselves and their children. Out of this failure in pluralism, the family lost its inner balance and condition of intergenerational respect. It is in this way that the phenomenon Phillippe Ariès argued for the nineteenth century families of Britain and France may have been specially poignant and strong in the United States: the intense, private family may at this historical moment have worked to destroy the emotional power and the dignity of the people whom it sheltered.

11

UNION PARK FAMILIES AND

THE CULTURE OF INDUSTRIAL CITIES

The family has an enormous influence on men's lives, yet there exists little coherent knowledge of how it functions. The fault certainly comes not from a lack of research,[1] nor does the difficulty lie in the quality of the research, at least in sociological study of families. Sociologists in the main have scrutinized the family with a kind of moral concern and directness that is a refreshing change from the dry "objectivity" through which other areas of social life have been embalmed. The study of family structure and function has also, on the whole, been free of those self-conscious anxieties about methodological correctness so common a "job neurosis" of social scientists. The problems besetting current family studies are rather that they contribute parts to a nonexistent whole: researchers do not understand how family processes interact broadly with other elements in society, and how such interactions change as the family and other social forces change. There is, then, a lack of context for the family; one may speak of "urban" families or "mobile" families yet have no clear sense of what these words mean.

A large measure of the blame for this lack of context belongs to historians, for they have failed to provide students of modern families with any real idea of what is modern about the families studied. Even the nature of the family phenomena that should be subject to historical treatment has no clear form. The common argument that biological processes of the family are ahistorical and "other" processes are cultural has now, in the light of Phillippe Ariès' researches, to be discarded empirically as well as logically, since this idea that the family acts as a shelter until the individual is biologically able to act as a full adult turns out to involve a cultural presupposition of what the "biology" of the individual is.

For American families, the historical picture is particularly barren, the "great unknown" of American social development in Bernard Bailyn's words. Of disciplined studies on American family structure over time, there is Bailyn's own work, an exciting but preliminary study, there is the excellent work of Demos, some incidental essays by Oscar Handlin, the outdated and narrow history of Arthur Calhoun's, and a few other scattered studies.[2]

The effect of this darkness of the family's development is simple and trenchant. Studies of contemporary family life have few guides for judging what material is relevant to the family as an institution in and of itself, and what is relevant to the contemporary family as a historic force, working under a certain set of conditions, subject to change as those other conditions — such as urban form or class structure — change.

The lack of a time context in family studies requires that something be said of the Union Park families beyond the confines of their own experience. For their lives had an added cultural dimension in terms of what is known of families above and below them in the social structure of America at the time. Similarly, Union Park families had a distinctive relation to English middle class families of the period, and to what is known of family life in succeeding generations in America. The seemingly enormous task of cultural comparison is simplified by the fact that, apart from the contemporary situation, so little is known about any of these other large areas of family experience. If the lines of the present sketch are crude and bold, they are, at least, a design, and can be redrawn in the light of new research.

Union Park Families and the American Working Class

The position of the people of Union Park in the economic and social hierarchy of their time gave a particular character to their family experience, for the work and family patterns of social groups below and above were quite different.

One of the most graphic, incisive studies of the work patterns of poor families has, fortunately, been made for a time period close to the years examined in this study. Stephan Thernstrom's *Poverty and Progress* is an exploration of the mobility of unskilled laborers and their sons in Newburyport, Massachusetts, during a formative era of industrialization, 1850–1880. The book is an attempt to show the position of the very poor in a small industrial city, and an attempt also to clarify certain general misconceptions about the nature of social mobility in the proletariat, misconceptions largely traceable to Lloyd Warner's massive analysis of the same community in the 1930's.[3]

Thernstrom's methods were roughly comparable to the techniques of the Union Park study in that census data was analyzed for individuals and related to the city directories of Newburyport. Though his data on family characteristics was more restricted than that available for Union Park, the rigor of his investigation permits contrasts between family lives in a poor and a middle class community of the time.

Thernstrom found a slight, sharply limited pattern of upward mobility among the workers of industrial Newburyport, a mobility more pronounced for the sons of unskilled laborers than for unskilled laborers themselves. Among those fathers who were upwardly mobile into skilled crafts, some of their sons were able to achieve skilled status, but in almost all cases there was a "ceiling" of mobility so that it was very difficult for either generation to move into nonmanual labor of any kind.

Instead, gains by the generations of workers were ploughed into what Thernstrom calls a pattern of "property mobility," the acquisition of a home or of a small savings account. In order to make economic gains of this sort, working class families sacrificed future occupational mobility of their sons into middle class pursuits, by putting the sons to work as soon as possible rather than keeping them in school: "The ordinary workman of nineteenth century Newburyport could rarely build up a savings account and purchase a home with making severe sacrifices. To cut family consumption expenditures to the bone was one such sacrifice. To withdraw the children from school and to put them to work at the age of ten or twelve was another . . . the sons of exceptionally prosperous laborers did *not* enjoy generally superior career opportunities; the sacrifice of their education and the constriction of their occupational opportunities, in fact, was often a prime cause of the family's property mobility." [4] Acquisition of property, then, was the mobility route these workers took in lieu of entry into nonmanual work. What did it mean about the family lives of the workers themselves?

When this working class property mobility, involving

sons in a somewhat sacrificial role, is contrasted to the dominant family pattern of Union Park, it is striking how much greater cohesiveness existed in the working class families than in the middle class families. These unskilled and semiskilled laborers molded the careers of their sons in terms of worldly desires of their own; they were, as fathers, far stronger than middle class fathers in Union Park. The strength of Newburyport's fathers was authoritarian in nature, for the children were removed from school to work as soon as they were physically capable of doing manual labor. The sons were not, evidently, allowed the luxury of deciding whether or not to pursue more education or a chancy job experiment in hopes of boosting themselves, as individuals, into another stratum of life.

This image of the working class family hardly permits that romanticizing of "the poor" to which some intellectuals are so prone. The cohesive family styles Thernstrom discovered among the poor were not the result of simple emotional bonds; an additional element of what Lipset, in another context, has called "working-class authoritarianism" [5] was here present in a most brutal and intimate form, through the manner in which the possible future prospects of the young were sacrificed for the achievement of worldly goals of the father himself. The bleakness of the material lives of these people had an emotional character, then, as well, in the power relations that existed between generations within the family. The discontinuity between worldly experience of the generations in Union Park, where the fathers became weak and passive, was in working class Newburyport removed at the expense of the liberty of the sons.

This working class family pattern, no less than the experience of the middle class families of Union Park, marked a break from the preindustrial families of Tocqueville's day, for in Newburyport the freedom of the generations was denied by the kind of power a father exercised over his sons. If the father as a model, as a reference point, had become weak in the middle class families of Union Park, the sons of Newburyport's working class operated under restrictions that made them weak; they were denied the chance to start out in the world on their own.

Union Park and the American Upper Classes

American elite families have seldom been studied as families, but rather, in the mold of C. Wright Mills, as tools by which status is maintained. Part of the difficulty in studying some American elites is their proximity to the life styles of the middle class; Bernard Barber has commented that, in general, mobility from the middle class status of a father to the elite business status of a son is often an economic difference which will not indicate a shift in the values or power relationships within the family.[6]

This grey area between upper class and middle class life has not always existed; it could well be argued that status differences between the two groups have decreased over the course of the last half century, and that there has developed a more fluid movement from middle class to elite status.[7] The relation of Union Park's families to the elites of the time shows a greater divide a century ago.

The majority of the residents in Union Park in the years after the Great Fire were of a different sort from those who lived in the community in the halcyon years of the 1850's and 1860's. The new Union Park residents were respectable but not fashionable; the first generation had been among the leaders of Chicago society. However, that older upper class generation was itself in a process of change in the years after the Civil War. The asceticism of the Chatfield-Taylor home and others like it was being challenged by a more cosmopolitan, luxuriant style of life. It was this new style of American upper class behavior that came into its own during the decades when the middle classes lived in Union Park; in Chicago, wealthy people were now attending the operas, giving sumptuous balls, and even gambling, men and women together, in posh, private casinos.

Opposed to this life style was the middle class behavior Wilkie found among the Union Park people: sedate and ascetic, with impersonal church meetings and philanthropies for the women, occasional visits to the local club for the more prosperous man, a rigid propriety in the home — in short, dull and unsensual.

Why did this difference exist? Obviously, the middle classes were not aping the behavior and tone of the wealthy, as can be argued occurs now, but were living instead a restrictive life that had become unfashionable. The burghers of a community like Union Park were engaged in something different from a simple imitation of the people they saw above them.

Since a parallel situation existed in England at this time, it is useful to look at the same class relationship in that culture. In England the relations between the gentry and the middle groups might be called a duel between freedom and probity, where the gentry felt itself, by its superior station, free to live independently of the mores of the majority of Victorian England, to be as eccentric, as given over to pleasure, as individual as it wanted. This class behavior, points out W. J. Reader, was not simply a fanciful stereotype of the gentry but within them a deep-felt urge, one that sprung up as a way for the landowner to set himself apart from the ugliness of industrial England.[8] However, the middle classes, G. M. Young has written, used the rules of respectability as a weapon to establish their position of dominance in society. While they were immensely envious of the old-line gentry, they felt their righteousness, their purity of character, would give them a tool of status, a tool of equal dignity, with which to challenge the men whose predecessors led preindustrial England.[9]

Since there was lacking in America of the same time period a traditional upper class whose privileges and members were defined by lineal descent, a different set of causes must explain what looks to be a similar phenomenon. The dynamics of family life provided, in Union Park, the clue to understanding how the people of the community came to a similar value "orientation," a value put on respectability and self-asceticism.

It would be logical, if a man were immobile in a city society undergoing enormous change, for him to make a virtue of stability. If stability is good, then his own failure or unwillingness to grasp new opportunities in the world at large can be justified. In Union Park, the tool of this stability was the intensive family, but it was a tool also to be used against another class. For if the clerk or accountant, the small shopkeeper or salesman, had somehow failed to succeed in a culture putting the highest premium on success, and if he saw those who did succeed displaying their wealth, in the giving of balls and dinners, in buying costly gowns and dresses for their wives and daughters, in building lavish houses, it would be natural for that clerk or that salesman to justify himself by giving up such things supposedly of his own accord, by deciding they did not constitute the good life. Moderation and self-asceticism would be a defense against feeling the sting of having not succeeded in gaining material success; jealousy would be transmuted into self-righteousness.

The concept of middle-class "worldly asceticism" is of course a familiar one, for it is the life view Max Weber saw in those people under the web of the "Protestant ethic." [10] But this ethic of worldly asceticism has a varying historical context for the middle class, one appropriate to middle-class people who failed to be upwardly mobile in their lives, as well as appropriate for earlier, more mobile people. Therefore, instead of Weber's notion that worldly asceticism was the accumulation of goods to demonstrate moral virtue, it is more plausible that, in this industrial city, worldly asceticism, self-conscious inhibition of enjoyment, was a response to relative material failure to "make it": asceticism made a virtue of stability under conditions where other people were rich, or becoming rich.

In this way the divergence between the middle class culture of Union Park and the more cosmopolitan, material culture of the upper classes can be explained by the dynamics of the work experience of the Union Park people themselves. This self-conscious asceticism, a response to failure, found its medium in the sanctification of the family unit, and its target in those above the middle class whose wealth had somehow been bought at the price of "sensual corruption." This, too, was a familiar idea a little later in the Progressive Era,[11] but its roots were subtle, and reached into the structural experiences of family and work in the middle classes themselves.

Modern-day research on the recruitment of business elites in the late nineteenth century shows that some of the small group at the top of society was originally drawn from the upper middle classes, though, because the upper middle classes were numerically larger, few of their numbers became elite.[12] In the main, those who were elite in the small towns or cities of America continued to dominate the elites of the industrial order.[13] In Union Park, few of the executive group became elite, though the elite drew from this group rather than lower down in society, the rags to riches ideal being very rarely realized. At the same time, maintaining "executive status," at the upper middle class level, was a precarious undertaking for the dominant family group, with less than half the executives in 1880 being able to maintain themselves at their status for a decade.

This bourgeois asceticism was thus plausibly a defense against cultural differences from above. What about the fate of those, within the middle classes, who were culturally different? Thernstrom found that in the working classes foreign birth or foreign parentage played a crippling role in occupational mobility, though not in accumulating property.[14] The foreign family suffered a similar occupational difficulty in the middle class homes of Union Park.

Ethnicity and Social Mobility in Union Park

The findings for the foreign-born in Union Park are of special interest because the native and foreign populations were residentially integrated. If such commonality serves to break down cultural barriers, as many Americans have hoped for in integrating housing between races, the data ought to have shown at least some signs that the children of culturally diverse neighborhoods could achieve similar patterns of worldly success. Unhappily, in Union Park, residential integration did not produce this outcome.

There were not enough foreign families in the tracing sample with characteristics working against intensity to make usable comparisons between intensive and less intensive families, though the proportions of native and foreigner were the same in the tracing as in the Census. Like the great majority of all people in Union Park, most foreign families were of an intensive type; the tracing did reveal, however, a group of differences between natives and foreigners within the intensive family itself.

Foreign-born fathers had a quite variable work experience, more unstable than that of the native-born in establishing class positions over the course of time. During some periods in the years from 1872 to 1890 they were more heterogeneous than native-born fathers; during other periods they came close to the profiles of the native-born family heads. The situation of the sons of the foreign-born was more clearcut. Starting from a base similar to that of the children from native families, they had a steadily worsening position in their occupational profiles, relative to sons of native-born fathers.

As Chicago became more commercially and industrially developed, then, young people from a different cultural background experienced difficulties in the middle classes parallel to the difficulties experienced by foreign-culture individuals in the working classes. What was striking about this development was that it did not lead to a pattern of residential separation; the foreigner and his sons, though experiencing difficulties in the work world of the native culture, did not retreat from living with native-born people. In contrast to ghetto conditions among the foreign-born who were poor, over the course of eighteen years fathers and sons from foreign backgrounds were exactly similar in their residence patterns to people from native homes. Further, the interspersing house by house of natives and foreigners, found in the 1880 Census, persisted over the course of time. The influence of middle class life on the relations between native and foreigner might exactly have consisted, in Union Park, in the capacity to sustain residential patterns of integration even as the work experience of the two groups diverged. This was perhaps a strange pattern of acceptance and mutuality between cultures, but it avoided, at least, that choking, that cutting off from the mainstream of American life, which so many children of the ghettoes were soon to experience.

Intensive Families and Work in the Present Day

The argument between Parsons and Ariès on the reasons for formation of intensive family life in the industrial era exists in a different form in discussion of modern-day nuclear and extended families. The Parsonian view is by no means the only point of view in the field of family studies, though it has had great influence, particularly in summarizing the group of family traits associated with family intensity under the rubric of "nuclear" structure. Bell and Vogel leave open the issue of the functional effectiveness of the nuclear family in terms of an "external" system like the work force; they point out simply the fact of nuclear families dominating the populations of the modern city.[15] William J. Goode takes the Parsonian view to a certain extent, but, unlike Parsons, Goode does not insist on the necessity of the "fit" between industrial city systems and the conjugal, or nuclear family: "Nevertheless, we cannot, in analyzing the interaction of the great social forces making for family change, presume some sort of natural "harmony" between the modern complex of industrialism and the conjugal (nuclear) family unit." This is because, Goode says, family and industrial factors are independent but interacting variables. Industrial forces, Goode believes, cannot "shape everything to their measure. The very *resistance* of family systems to such pressures indicates their independence as a set of forces."[16]

Another direction, independent of Parsons, and closely

aligned to the ideas of this study, has been taken by Miller and Swanson in their unfairly neglected book, *The Changing American Parent*. Miller and Swanson believe that a family nurturing based on intimacy and isolation of the family from the society around it was foreign to the demands made on family members during the period of "entrepreneurial" growth in the late nineteenth century. Miller and Swanson do not entertain the notion, advanced in this study, that such families of refuge would still be dominant under "entrepreneurial" conditions, precisely because the demands and human contacts of that social order were frightening. But their work does explore in depth for modern times how the processes of work in highly structured industrial society are related to sheltering, intimate, and intense families.[17]

For contemporary family structures, the arguments directed against the ideas of Parsons, and such followers of his as George Homans and Robert Schneider,[18] have two forms, both again narrowed to the question of kinship structure. One is the argument that extended families, such as defined in this study, with an outside kin member living in the residential household of the conjugal pair and their children, function as effectively, if not more effectively, than isolated nuclear family units. The work here of Michael Young and Peter Willmott is the most distinguished;[19] from the vantage point of the Union Park experience, their findings seem to point to a continuing modality of strength in extended families of this form.

The second attack on the Parsonian idea of nuclear family functional dominance is made by family researchers who explore a middle region between the nuclear and extended families as defined in this study; this middle region had been termed the "extended family cohesion" that exists between related nuclear families. The basic argument here is that there is beneficial mutual assistance and support between groups of related nuclear families who live, nonetheless, residentially apart from each other, and this cohesion is, for the families themselves, an end in itself. In this school the role of family size comes into play, then, in a subtle way as well.

To understand the human relevance of this second academic attack on the Parsonians, and its relation to the Union Park findings, it is necessary to know what in Parsons' theory is challenged by existence of cohesion between nuclear family units. The critique is spelled out clearly in an excellent "note" on extended family and urban society, by Allen Coult and Robert Habenstein, in *The Sociological Quarterly*.[20] Parsons assumes, they point out, the nuclear family would function so that "universalistic requirements of the society are transmitted to the child." Translated from the sociologese, this means no small group institution or loyalty would bind the child and young man so that he would resist participating in the widest range of social activities to develop his own social or psychic potential; for instance, the child would not grow up feeling such loyalty to a particular locality or to a particular family group that he would be unwilling to break away for the sake of realizing something within himself. In this way the "universalism" of the social fabric, where none of the parts have an organic life of their own that can hold the individual, is compatible with the greatest degree of individualism. Parsons' theory, on this account, resembles John Stuart Mill's concept of the ideal liberty of a person in modern society.

But this concept of universalism, of liberation from particular loyalties, is challenged when families operate so that one end of family life is cooperation and mutual support between nuclear units, with individuals sacrificing part of their own time, or money, or emotional energy, for the sake of a familial unit in which they as individuals are submerged. Cohesion between nuclear families, the second definition of extended family relations, should break down the economic integration and social mobility of the people involved were the Parsonian theory to hold, but the bulk of recent studies seem to show that where this family cohesion exists, there is greater upward mobility.

The arguments for the existence of effective, functional cohesion between urban nuclear families sort themselves into subsets of thought, one arguing simply that the cohesion exists and is associated with mobile family groups, the other going much further by arguing that the "isolated" nuclear family is simply a "fiction," a misleading stereotype. The first school of thought develops from the excellent researches of Eugene Litwak and Marvin Sussman.[21] Though an empirical challenge to their work can be found in the researches of Robert Stuckert,[22] researches which are in line with the Parsonian hypothesis, the greater scope, larger samples, and, not least, superior analysis in the Litwak and Sussman studies makes them the more convincing.

On the basis of these studies, there would seem to be real deficiencies in the Parsonian description of the family. In terms of people's lives, the middle class families of the modern city seem to have achieved a subtle, and highly civilized, network of kinship ties; there is mutual economic assistance in time of trouble or sickness, help in occupational achievement, or sharing between families, yet the individuality of each conjugal unit is maintained, so that a concurrent private and corporate family life is possible. How did this state of affairs come to be, what are the influences that would generate such a family situation in the modern city?

The question becomes important when we consider the second subset of thought on the nature of cohesion of nuclear families; this school is represented by Marvin Sussman's "The Isolated Nuclear Family: Fact or Fiction," [23] and Sussman's work is related explicitly and logically to the challenge Scott Greer makes to the idea of the isolation and anomie of the individual in the modern city. Sussman takes the position in this article that cohesion between nuclear units not only exists, and is instrumentally effective, but that it is the normative form of relationships between families. The isolation of the nuclear family may occur, but not as a major mode of family life. Sussman then asks, why does one find the great sociologists of the late nineteenth and early twentieth centuries, Durkheim, Simmel, Tönnies, Mannheim, describing the family in just the opposite way? This is the same problem Scott Greer poses about ideas of the psychic isolation of the individual in the city.[24]

Sussman accounts for the differences in one of two possible ways: either there is a "theory-research lag" between the time of the great theorists and the present, or the urban family itself has changed in the course of the last century. Sussman's second proposal has the advantage, in addition to its modesty, of the concord it would bring between the data like that on the Union Park families and the data on the modern-day cohesion between nuclear families. A century ago middle class families such as these people in Chicago were described by sociologists to be isolated and, in Durkheim's phrase, anomic — lost in the city.

Does this comparison of the first industrial-urban nuclear families with the present mean that the people studied in Union Park were "sports," a temporary aberration of demographic dominance that occurred simply in response to the first shocks of industrialization?

This would be a tempting summary of their experience if only there could be put aside the widespread psychological concern, as reported in the works of Erikson and Keniston, with the unequal balance of power between fathers and mothers in many modern middle class families. It was possible to explain how this "historical discontinuity" as Erikson calls it, was strongly related to what the Union Park people experienced, as a change that crystallized during their generation. But if the discontinuity has persisted, as Erikson and Keniston believe it has, if the psychic inequality between father and mother continues to leave a peculiar mark on many middle class American families, then the experience of the Union Park people was not a first-generation urban aberration.

Thus the question of the historical significance of the Union Park families resolves itself to the problem of explaining why families seem to have lost their isolated structure in the modern city over the last century, while the psychic conditions associated with this isolation continue to permeate some segments of family life.

Part of the explanation lies simply in the fact that isolation is a difficult mode of existence for people to bear. It may be necessary as a defense mechanism when a people experiences some great and unprecedented change like the building of an industrial city, but once the shock of the event has subsided, once related families have moved to the city over the course of time, or kin networks through one's children's marriages have been established, mutuality between nuclear families should develop.

But the character of this mutuality is quite different than that of the extensive families who existed in Union Park. An examination of the kind of help Sussman found between nuclear units in his Cleveland study clarifies the character of cohesion between modern nuclear families. The assistance most prevalent between the generations in the nuclear families and between the family and all other kin was help during illness; this was followed by financial aid, occasional care of children, the giving of personal and business advice, and finally the giving of valuable gifts. But with the historical perspectives that the Union Park data afford, these findings in Cleveland take on a rather different significance than Sussman allows them.[25]

It will be recalled that when Tocqueville looked at the American family, he perceived an enormous amount of advice flowing from fathers to their children, and that such advice constituted the foundation of respect the sons had for their nonauthoritarian fathers. In Union Park, a discontinuity in the work experience of fathers and sons, coming from the intensive fathers' immobility in the face of the city's growth, logically broke this flow of accepted advice from father to son, for the fathers had an experience, a noncoping one, much different from their sons in facing the same problems, and so lost their capacities to act and speak as models for action.

In this light, Sussman's findings look a little different. Only a quarter of his respondents indicated receiving significant advice from their parents, and a much smaller proportion, 3 percent, of the respondents indicated giving significant personal or business advice to their own children. The greatest area of help is one that would occur during an emergency, when someone was ill, something out of the routine of family life.

Sussman's findings, interpreted this way, suggest that now there is a sense of family obligation under conditions of stress in these Cleveland homes, but that the psychic mutuality between family groups is much more limited, that people still do not "interfere" in their children's lives with advice, even though the children, beneath a veneer of independence, might want and need it.

Analysis of another of Sussman's categories makes this even more apparent. Nearly half of his respondents indicated that they had received financial help from their parents; this would make sense given the fact that much of this adult generation was nurtured or reached adulthood during the Great Depression of the 1930's. But only 10 percent of the respondents indicated giving financial support to their own children (and only 14 percent indicated giving financial support to their parents). The generation of adults Sussman studied evidently gave its children little more concrete financial help than it did personal or business advice.

I do not mean to imply Sussman did his work poorly — quite the contrary, his family studies are impressive pieces of research. But the materials of his study show something peculiar to modern families. In contrast to the families of Union Park, as I read their experience, these modern families have reasserted the sense of family *obligation* between nuclear units, especially during times of stress like family illness or economic disaster, but that the sense of emotional rapport, of advice-giving and advice-taking, that once constituted the basis of respect between the younger and the older generation, may be as concretely absent here as in Union Park. In this way, the observations of father-weakness of Erikson and Keniston can be brought into line with the structural conditions noted by Sussmann and Litwak. The *instrumental* bonds between nuclear families may have re-established themselves over the course of the last century, but the primary, emotional bonds between male generations may be recurrently weak, so that a sense of the father's absence as a positive force in his son's life could occur as the psychologists describe it. In this way, a structural break in the family occurring in the Union Park generation could have passed down psychologically in the country's history, even though the structural conditions of the family have evolved into a new form.

That there was something in these Union Park families resonant with the discontents of comfortable families of our own time struck me from the moment I began to pore over the traces of their lives. If the conclusions drawn in this study from their history and from the mute figures of their lives are correct, then these people, distant from us as they are, may have inaugurated a pattern of family conduct that has culminated in the intense family life of modern suburbs, now coming to so sorry a fruition. The present does not duplicate the past; the work experience of modern generations is different, and the suburbs of the modern middle classes surely experience a different kind of isolation from the city center from that which the Union Park people experienced. And yet the impulse to retreat from disorder, to make of the family a bulwark against confusion, rather than the center of a full range of human experience, may persist across time. If the young men fresh from World War II and the Depression responded to this impulse, and sought in their neat suburban ranch houses and split-levels a shelter from the trials of their youth, then the family disease the Union Park people suffered may be upon many Americans again, and may explain something of the gulf now opened between fathers and sons.

TECHNICAL APPENDIX

NOTES

INDEX

TECHNICAL APPENDIX:

ANALYSIS OF THE CENSUS MATERIALS

The statistical materials used in this study were the census records for 1880 on a forty-block section of the near West side. The forty blocks covered, west to east, the Union Park residences to the commercial boundary of the Haymarket; north to south, the census mapping ran from the edge of a frame-house and storage area to the edge of a similar frame-house area to the south. The mapped area in between consisted for the most part of brick residences.

Microfilmed copies of each handwritten household census report for the people in this T-shaped section were coded and processed through the Data-Text System, a new computer language for social science.[1] The census reports contained information on each household unit in the area, its structural composition, and each of the individuals within it; the processing of census materials was on all three of these levels.

The primitive technology at the time these census documents were collected meant that statisticians could do little more than count up the number of people in each of the categories. The

[1] Used through the courtesy of Harvard Computing Center and Professor Arthur S. Couch.

cross-tabulations performed by the computer did not, therefore, duplicate any of the materials published at the time on the basis of this data; in fact, most of the items in these census reports were not even analyzed by the writers of the census reports for 1880.[2]

A GLOSSARY OF CENSUS TERMS AND CATEGORIES

Census Family: All individuals in the census manuscripts were organized into family units. Thus if four *unrelated* families lived at one address, the people at that address were organized as four separate groups, rather than as one "household."

Census Family Head: In each family, one person, usually the person who carried the major economic burdens of the family, was designated the "head of household"; in a small family, this was usually the father, and in a family where grandfather, father, and adult sons were found, it was usual, again, for the father to be assigned the designation "head of household."

Occupation: The census employed no standard list of occupations, but recorded whatever occupational label a person ascribed to himself; this variety of occupations was reduced here to about 200 different forms of work.

Unemployed-Employed: The census takers were required to ask, of any persons in the household who listed themselves as working during 1880, how many months, if any, they were unemployed during the year. The census takers in the Union Park locality did not note the number of months of unemployment, but instead made a check mark if at some point during the year the person was unemployed. Thus, temporary periods of inactivity due to job change are interspersed with people who were out of work for some time.

Nativity: The census required that every native-born respondent list the state in which he was born, and the state in

[2] See, for example, 18th Census of the United States, 1880, vol. 18, *Social Statistics of Cities.*

which his parents were born; for those born abroad, or whose parents were born abroad, the nationality was sufficient.

THE CODING OF THE 1880 CENSUS

Professional readers who can make further use of the census materials are referred to the coding scheme for this study on file at the Joint Center for Urban Studies, 66 Church Street, Cambridge, Mass. A complete set of cross-tabulations used in the preparation of this book is also on file there.

CHICAGO IN 1880

To evaluate the character of the census materials of 1880, it is necessary to know the state of prosperity in Chicago as a whole at the time when the census was taken.

A narrative of the year 1880 in Chicago would make dull but untroubled reading. Nothing of the scale of the Great Fire or the labor riots of 1873 occurred; the most exciting event of the year was the presidential election in the fall, and even that stirred little excitement. In a review of the year, compiled by the *Chicago Tribune,* and published on January 1 of the new year, 1881, the tone was one of satisfaction with the economic and social state of the city, and relief that the stresses of the Depression of 1873–1879 had now passed. "The past year has been the most prosperous of all the years of our city, and as such its history has a special importance for our own people; but, being as it is the centre of the most prosperous section of the country, being unrivaled in its growth and progress, this year's history cannot but have peculiar interest for non-residents of Chicago." But this general prosperity had a peculiar quality: it was not "wildly illusive as was the apparent prosperity of the years following the war and preceding the panic." Speculative enterprises the *Tribune* saw in this year as of "a more legitimate and conservative character."

In addition to the character of the speculation made in this year, prosperity had been advanced by three other factors: the growing bullion supplies of the country, the enlargement of the bank-note circulation, and the renewed inflow of capital from abroad.

The result of this renewal of the capital base was, in Chicago, the following: the volume of trade in the city increased 23⅓ percent over 1879, and the productive output of the city's industries gained an average 15 percent, with special gains in meat-packing and iron processing. Modern-day economists would certainly disagree with this simple conjunction of renewed capital base to renewed productivity and trade — while being unable among themselves to agree on an alternate model — but to the editors of the *Tribune* effects of this economic prosperity were palpable: "The labor market has received a wonderful stimulus, workers having been really scarce in not a few instances, and the number of those wanting to work, but not able to obtain employment, has been reduced to a smaller percentage than at any other time since the close of the War."

Similarly, the influx of immigrants into Chicago in this year was directly correlated, the *Tribune* believed, to the character of the economic renewal of the city. As a result of the decrease in immigration during the years of the depression and the subsequent increase in 1880 when prosperity returned to the city, "the problem of immigration is not now so perplexing as it was considered to be before the panic, for our experience with hard times has proved that immigration regulates itself, and that there is little danger of more people coming to this country than the country is prepared to receive and utilize." The influx of immigrants during this year of recovery, says the *Tribune,* had, in turn, a "salutary and important influence" in discouraging labor strikes and other worker outbursts that might have occurred were there a marked scarcity of cheap labor, and so a temptation to the workers to press demands. The year, indeed, has been free of such "embarrassments."

The *Tribune* summed up the state of urban prosperity as follows: "We have thus enjoyed a season of unusual prosperity which has ramified down into the most minute features of city life, giving to retailer as well as wholesale dealer, to the worker as well as the capitalist, the full benefit of prosperous times."

NOTES

CHAPTER ONE

1. Carter Harrison, "Memoirs," in Caroline Kirkland, ed., *Chicago Yesterdays, A Sheaf of Reminiscences* (Chicago: Daughaday and Company, 1919), p. 174.

2. H. C. Chatfield-Taylor, *Chicago* (Boston: Houghton Mifflin, 1917), p. 49.

3. Harrison in Kirkland, *Chicago Yesterdays*, p. 174.

4. Anon., *Chicago's First Half-Century* (Chicago: The Inter-Ocean Publishing Co., 1883), p. 29.

5. John W. Reps, *The Making of Urban America* (Princeton: Princeton University Press, 1965), p. 300.

6. Charles Cleaver, *Reminiscences of Chicago during the Forties and Fifties* (Chicago: Fergus Publishing Co., 1913), pp. 55–56.

7. Homer Hoyt, *One Hundred Years of Land Values in Chicago* (Chicago: University of Chicago Press, 1933), p. 42; *Chicago Land Use Survey,* Community Area No. 28 (Chicago: Chicago Plan Commission, 1940), p. 2.

8. Hoyt, *One Hundred Years,* p. 42.

9. Chicago *Daily News,* May 12, 1923, pp. 2–3.

10. Hoyt, *One Hundred Years,* p. 91.

11. One factor of this linear phenomenon was the planning and final opening of three streetcar lines (horse driven then, of course) in Chicago in 1859, a mode of transport to replace the old omnibuses. The West Side lines — and there were two of these compared to one each for the South and North Sides — flowed directly to the central business district from the community around Union Park. The North Side line began above the river; the South Side line touched the

central business district at a point little developed at that time. Only the West Side lines afforded transit to all of the business district, and direct transit from all parts of this district out again to a residential area. See Hoyt, *One Hundred Years*, pp. 77–78.

12. Harrison, in Kirkland, *Chicago Yesterdays*, p. 154.

13. Reps, *The Making of Urban America*, pp. 325–338.

14. M. H. Putney, *Real Estate Values and Historical Notes of Chicago* (Chicago, 1900), p. 116; illustrations in Chatfield-Taylor between pp. 54–55 and in vol. 3 of A. T. Andreas, *History of Chicago* (3 volumes; Chicago: A. T. Andreas Co., 1886).

15. *U.S. Census,* 1890, vol. 18, p. 496.

16. Harrison in Kirkland, *Chicago Yesterdays,* p. 169.

17. Harrison in Kirkland, *Chicago Yesterdays,* p. 177.

18. Chatfield-Taylor, *Chicago,* pp. 55–56.

19. Oscar Handlin, *The Americans* (Boston: Little-Brown, 1963), p. 277.

20. Chatfield-Taylor, *Chicago,* p. 58.

21. Chatfield-Taylor, *Chicago,* pp. 57–60.

22. Chatfield-Taylor, *Chicago,* pp. 55–56.

23. *Ibid.*

24. For a picture of this newer generation see Herma Clark, *The Elegant Eighties* (Chicago: A. C. McClurg, 1941).

25. Harrison in Kirkland, *Chicago Yesterdays,* pp. 172, 162–163.

26. Harrison in Kirkland, *Chicago Yesterdays,* p. 174.

27. Harrison in Kirkland, *Chicago Yesterdays,* pp. 164–165.

28. Harrison in Kirkland, *Chicago Yesterdays,* pp. 172, 174.

29. Harrison in Kirkland, *Chicago Yesterdays,* pp. 165–166.

30. Chicago *Daily News,* May 12, 1923, p. 12.

31. See Hull House Maps in *Hull House Maps and Papers,* by residents of Hull House (New York: Thomas Y. Crowell, 1895).

32. See Harrison in Kirkland, *Chicago Yesterdays,* pp. 170–171, and Chicago *Daily News,* May 12, 1923, p. 12.

33. John G. Gawelti, *Apostles of the Self-made Man* (Chicago: University of Chicago Press, 1964), pp. 162–163.

34. C. S. Winslow, *Historical Events of Chicago* (Chicago: Chicago Historical Society, 1967), II, 38.

CHAPTER TWO

1. James Burnley, *Millionaires and Kings of Enterprise* (London: Harmsworth Bros., Ltd., 1901), pp. 416–417.

2. Anon., "Potter Palmer: Five Biographical Sketches by Friends" (unpublished manuscript written as a memoriam, Chicago Historical Society, 1902), p. B.

3. Edward F. Dunne, *Illinois, Heart of the Nation* (Chicago: Lewis Co., 1933), p. 454.

4. Burnley, *Millionaires,* p. 418; Anon., "Potter Palmer: Five Biographical Sketches by Friends," pt. E, A–B. See also Chicago *Daily News,* May 12, 1923, p. 12.

5. See Robert H. Wiebe's excellent *The Search for Order* (New York: Hill and Wang, 1967), chapters 1 and 2, for a discussion of this phenomenon at the national level.

6. Winslow, *Historical Events of Chicago,* II, 137; Anon., *Biographical Dictionary of Chicago* (Chicago, n.d.), II, 704.

7. *Historical Events of Chicago,* II, 137; *Biographical Dictionary of Chicago,* II, 704.

8. Burnley, *Millionaires,* p. 420.

9. Hoyt, *One Hundred Years,* p. 90.

10. *Ibid.*

11. Chicago *Daily News,* May 12, 1923, p. 12.

12. Part of the complaint of citizens of the West Side about their post–Civil War position in the city concerned the site for Lincoln Park, eventually located near the North Side. This park, like those of the earlier period, was thought to attract transportation facilities, and thus help the residents in its neighborhood. A poor discussion of this is found in Edward T. Kirkland, *Story of Chicago* (Chicago, 1892), pp. 276–277.

13. Chatfield-Taylor, *Chicago,* p. 63.

14. Chicago *American,* May 17, 1954; Chicago *Sun Times,* September 23, 1955.

15. Chicago *Sun Times,* September 23, 1955; Hoyt, *One Hundred Years,* p. 102; *Chicago Land Use Survey,* p. 2.

16. Hoyt, *One Hundred Years,* pp. 102–103.

17. Burnley, *Millionaires,* p. 420.

18. Robert Wiebe, *The Search for Order,* pp. 18–19.

19. See Stephan Thernstrom, *Poverty and Progress* (Cambridge: Harvard University Press, 1964) for an excellent discussion of this phenomenon in another city.

20. Hoyt, *One Hundred Years,* p. 125.

21. Hoyt, *One Hundred Years,* p. 138.

22. *Ibid.*

23. Such protection was one of the purposes of the Burnham Plan at the turn of the century.

24. This estimate is based on earlier ward records used in the 1860 Census, on file at the Chicago Historical Society, and on the amount of unburned land mass on the near West Side.

25. Henry Nash Smith, ed., *Popular Culture and Industrialism* (Garden City: Doubleday and Company, 1967), documents 42–45.

26. Smith, *Popular Culture,* documents 39 and 40.

27. U.S. Department of Commerce and the Bureau of the Census,

Historical Statistics of the United States, Colonial Times to the Present (Washington, D.C., 1950), pp. 12–13. The Union Park data was compared to these general figures.

CHAPTER THREE

1. "Letters and Reminiscences of Laura Kendall Thomas" (in the library of the the Chicago Historical Society), p. 1.

2. White collar earnings averaged about $1000 a year, and rent averaged between 30 and 40 percent of that figure — see discussion of such balances in Simon Kuznets, *Modern Economic Growth* (New Haven: Yale University Press, 1966), chapters 4 and 5.

3. "Letters and Reminiscences," pp. 1–2.

4. F. B. Wilkie, *Walks about Chicago* (Chicago: Belford, Clarke and Company, 1882), pp. 14, 20.

5. Wilkie, *Walks about Chicago,* pp. 19–20.

6. Theodore Dreiser, *Sister Carrie* (New York, 1900); see chapters four and six for the scenes from which this description was drawn.

7. "Potter Palmer: Five Biographical Sketches by Friends," p. 21.

8. On this era, see Herma Clark, *The Elegant Eighties.*

9. Herma Clark, *The Elegant Eighties,* Preface.

10. See Scott Greer, et al., *The New Urbanization* (New York: St. Martin's Press, 1968), for studies oriented along this line.

11. Chicago *Daily Tribune,* June 21, 1890, p. 1.

12. Chicago *Daily Tribune,* October 24, 1890, p. 1, and November 14, 1890, p. 2.

13. Chicago *Daily Tribune,* November 14, 1890, p. 6.

14. The signs of this development are still evident today. If one walks along Lake Street or Randolph, one sees warehouse after warehouse whose marker stones date from the 1890's or early 1900's until suddenly, on the western side of Halstead Street, older marble-fronts and brownstones stand out between the giant storage buildings.

CHAPTER FOUR

1. See Talcott Parsons and Robert Bales, *The Family: Socialization and Interaction Process* (Glencoe, Illinois: Free Press, 1955), esp. chapter one. Other phases of Parsons' work on the family are cited in the text below. Phillippe Ariès, *L'Enfant et la vie familiale sous l'ancien regime* (Paris: Libraire Plon, 1960), translated into English as *Centuries of Childhood* (New York: Vintage Books, 1965).

CHAPTER FIVE

1. Lynn Lees, "The Irish in London," unpublished manuscript prepared under the auspices of the Joint Center for Urban Studies, Cambridge, Mass. I should like to thank the author for sharing her materials on this question with me.

2. W. J. Goode, *The Family* (Englewood Cliffs, New Jersey, 1964), contains a good discussion of kinship terminology (pp. 51–52).

3. W. E. B. Dubois, *The Philadelphia Negro* (New York, edition of 1967), p. 166; Stephan Thernstrom, unpublished manuscript on social mobility in Boston, in preparation at the Joint Center for Urban Studies, Cambridge, Mass. I wish to thank Mr. Thernstrom for communicating his data on Boston to me.

4. Dubois, *The Philadelphia Negro*, pp. 164, 166; for a contrary argument see A. F. Weber, *The Growth of Cities in the Nineteenth Century* (Ithaca: Cornell University Press Reprint Series, 1963), pp. 336–337.

5. DuBois, *The Philadelphia Negro*, pp. 176, 177. These are figures from middle class Negro families: DuBois found them trying to live as much like their white neighbors as possible. DuBois' work contains the only solid data we have on middle class budgeting.

6. Compiled from data presented in the *1890 Census, Report on Manufacturing Industries*, Part II, *Statistics of Cities*, pp. 130–133.

7. Citywide figures compiled from the *10th Census of the United States*, 1880, vol. 19, sec. 2; *Social Statistics of Cities*, pp. 511–513.

8. The materials on Boston come from a communication of Stephan Thernstrom on his unpublished work on Boston laborers previously referred to; those in Philadelphia from DuBois, *The Philadelphia Negro*, p. 100.

9. Weber, *The Growth of Cities in the 19th Century*, p. 347.

10. See D. O. Price, "Needed Statistics for Minority Groups in Metropolitan Areas," and other papers in *Joint Center Conference on Social Statistics and the City* (Washington, D.C., Joint Center for Urban Studies, 1967).

11. Historical Statistics of the United States, p. 72.

12. Weber, *The Growth of Cities in the Nineteenth Century*, pp. 276–280.

CHAPTER SIX

1. Kingsley Davis and Lloyd Warner, "Structural Analysis of Kinship," *American Anthropologist*, April 1937; Talcott Parsons, "The Kinship System of the Contemporary United States," *Essays in Sociological Theory* (Glencoe, Illinois: Free Press, 1954); Erik Erikson, *Childhood and Society* (New York: W. W. Norton, 1950), pt. 3, and Erikson, "Growth and Crisis of the Healthy Personality," *Psychological Issues*, vol. 1, no. 1 (1959); Sigmund Freud, *Three Contributions to the Theory of Sex* (in *Complete Works of Sigmund Freud*; London: Hogarth Press, n.d.).

2. See S. N. Eisenstadt, *From Generation to Generation* (Glencoe, Illinois: Free Press, 1956), chapter 1, for a discussion of the theory of "age homogeneous" grouping which is used here.

3. *Historical Statistics,* p. 207. This applies to young people entering their eighteenth year, or younger. The percentage of those over 18 who acquired degrees was little higher.

4. This family phenomenon has been most fully described in biographies of artists, such as André Maurois' superb study of Balzac; one is always struck in these accounts by the large numbers of unartistic but cultured young men who drifted in Paris or Berlin with these writers or painters for a few years and then settled into a career; see also Erikson, *Childhood and Society,* "The Legend of Hitler's Youth."

5. It should be recalled that the census was coded so that those who did not list themselves as heads of households were also living in the same house with someone who was so listed; this means there were no situations in which a young man living in this Chicago neighborhood could list his parents in New York as the head of his household. If he lived alone, he was taken to be a unit all by himself.

6. *Historical Statistics,* p. 15.

7. *Ibid.*

8. Weber, *The Growth of Cities in the Nineteenth Century,* p. 342.

9. In his study of poor blacks in Philadelphia of the time, DuBois concluded that late marriages among the lower classes were of a different order and the result of instability in the family bond itself. (DuBois, *The Philadelphia Negro,* pp. 69–70).

10. The hidden rate of broken marriages is higher, as shall be shown later in the chapter, but the value put on marriage, as an institution, is revealed in this absence of official divorce.

11. Weber, *The Growth of Cities in the Nineteenth Century,* p. 341.

12. Oscar Handlin, *Race and Nationality in American Life* (Garden City, New Jersey: Anchor Books, 1957), p. 120.

13. *Ibid.,* p. 122.

14. *Ibid.*

15. *Ibid.*

16. *Ibid.,* p. 119.

17. Parsons and Bales, *Family, Socialization and Interaction,* pp. 4–6.

18. Lees, "The Irish in London"; this data I owe, again, to the kindness of the author in sharing her London Census materials with me.

CHAPTER SEVEN

1. Engels, *The Origin of the Family, Private Property, and the State,* trans. F. Untermann (Chicago: Charles Kerr and Co., 1902).

2. See Part B of Appendix to the 1880 Census for a description of Chicago's condition in 1880.

3. In this way ambiguities of sex roles, power relations in the family, and the like, found in such definitions of work orientation as Weber's "Protestant ethic" are avoided.

4. See William J. Goode, "Marital Satisfaction and Instability," in Lipset and Bendix, eds., *Class, Status, and Power* (second ed., Glencoe, Illinois: Free Press, 1966), pp. 381–387, for a discussion of the inverse relation between class and people who become alone through divorce, a relationship different from that posited earlier in the century. In a similar way, the early theorists believed that a lone, "free" man was more likely to be a successful entrepreneur because he was not tied down.

5. Lipset and Bendix, *Social Mobility in Industrial Society* (Berkeley: University of California Press, 1959), pp. 3–8, is a good discussion of more general impulses to mobility.

6. Lipset and Bendix, *Social Mobility and Industrial Society,* pp. 254–255.

7. See Anselm Strauss, *The Image of the City* (Glencoe, Illinois: Free Press, 1961), and Morton and Lucia White, *The Intellectual Versus the City* (Cambridge: Harvard University Press, 1962).

8. See Pitirim Sorokin, *Urban-Rural Sociology* (New York: Holt and Co., 1929).

CHAPTER EIGHT

1. The use of even-numbered years also had its positive side, for it increased the "penumbra" of possible time covered to 1871 and 1891; the span of time traced might best be called eighteen years mapped in regular half-steps, with a possible twenty-year reach.

CHAPTER NINE

1. See John Cawelti, *Apostles of the Self-Made Man* (Chicago: University of Chicago Press, 1965).

2. Reinhardt Bendix, *Work and Authority in Industry* (New York: Harper Torchbook edition, Harper and Row, 1963), pp. 254–273.

3. See B. L. Pierce, *Chicago* (New York: Alfred A. Knopf, 1957), vol. II, for a detailed but rather amorphous account of these years.

4. We have distinguished tables that traced individuals directly, called linked tables, and tables that showed changing concentration of population in certain social groups, called distributive tables. Since all of the trace sample lived in Union Park in 1880, movements out of the area after 1880 and into the area prior to 1880 were direct trace of individuals, though their format is that of the distributive

tables. For example, if 44 percent of the trace sample lived elsewhere in Chicago by 1890, this was a direct movement of 44 percent of the population over the course of the decade, since all the people in the trace sample lived in the community in 1880. By contrast, if 44 percent of the Union Park population in 1880 were skilled workers and 22 percent were skilled workers in 1890, this does not mean the other 22 percent found better or worse jobs; they may have moved out of the city, or all of the original number may be executives and their ranks filled to half by downward movement from other occupational groups. The unity of residence in 1880 made all population movements from this year, by contrast, indicators of linked, direct history of individuals.

5. See my "Middle-class Families and Urban Violence" in *Nineteenth Century Cities,* edited by Stephan Thernstrom and Richard Sennett (New Haven: Yale University Press, 1969).

CHAPTER TEN

1. Erik Erikson, *Childhood and Society* (New York: W. W. Norton Co., 1950), p. 295.

2. Alexis de Tocqueville, *Democracy in America* (trans. by Reeves, Bowen, and Bradley; New York: Vintage Press, 1960), II, 204, 202.

3. Tocqueville, pp. 205–206.

4. Wishy, *The Child and the Republic,* chap. 3.

5. William R. Taylor, *Cavalier and Yankee* (New York: Doubleday and Company, 1963, Anchor Edition), p. 24.

6. See Yehoshua Arieli, *Individualism and Nationalism in American Ideology* (Cambridge: Harvard University Press, 1964), esp. chapter IX.

7. Erikson, *Childhood and Society,* p. 296.

8. See Anselm Strauss, *Images of the American City* (Glencoe, Illinois: The Free Press, 1961), for an excellent discussion of this; also L. and M. White, *The American Intellectual Versus the City.*

9. Frank Lloyd Wright, *Autobiography* (New York: Duell, Sloan, and Pierce, 1943), p. 63.

10. See Sam B. Warner, Jr., *Streetcar Suburbs* (Cambridge: Harvard University Press, 1962), for excellent descriptive material.

11. The imagery of the Victorian family is discussed in W. J. Reader, *Life in Victorian England* (New York: Capricorn Edition, 1964), pp. 132–143; a specially striking instance of this family image occurs in Thackeray's *Vanity Fair,* in the kind of tragedy Rawdon Crawley finally understands to have occurred to his own family.

12. John Cawelti, *Apostles of the Self-made Man* (Chicago: University of Chicago Press, 1965), chap. 4.

13. I wish to thank Sam Bass Warner, Jr., for clarifying this issue for me.

14. David Aberle and Kaspar Naegele, "Middle-Class Fathers' Occupational Role and Attitudes toward Children," in Robert Bell and Ezra Vogel, eds., *A Modern Introduction to the Family* (Glencoe, Illinois: Free Press, 1960).

15. Eisenstadt, *From Generation to Generation* (Glencoe, Illinois: Free Press, 1956), p. 44.

16. See particularly Lifton's recent work on Hiroshima, *Death in Life* (New York: Random House, Inc., 1968).

17. Oscar and Mary F. Handlin, *The Dimensions of Liberty* (Cambridge: Harvard University Press, 1962).

18. See *Classic Essays on the Culture of Cities,* ed. with an Introduction by Richard Sennett (New York: Appleton-Century-Crofts, 1969), Introductory Essay, for a further discussion of the Chicago School's ideas for urban pluralism.

CHAPTER ELEVEN

1. See, for example, the massive Bibliographic Appendix in Nelson N. Foote and Leonard Cottrell, *Identity and Interpersonal Competence* (Chicago: University of Chicago Press, 1955).

2. Bernard Bailyn, *Education in the Forming of American Society* (Chapel Hill: University of North Carolina Press, 1960), pt. I; Handlin, *Race and Nationality in American Life* and *The Uprooted* (Cambridge: Harvard University Press, 1939); Arthur Calhoun, *A Social History of the Family* (New York, 1917); John Demos, "Notes on Life in Plymouth Colony," *William and Mary Quarterly,* 3rd ser., vol. 22, no. 2 (1965).

3. Stephan Thernstrom, *Poverty and Progress* (Cambridge: Harvard University Press, 1964); of the Yankee City series, the *Yankee City* (ed. Lloyd Warner; New Haven: Yale University Press, 1963), a one-volume abridged edition, is the clearest presentation of this classic work.

4. Thernstrom, p. 155.

5. See S. M. Lipset, *Political Man* (New York: Anchor Books Edition, 1963), chap. 4, "Working Class Authoritarianism."

6. See Bernard Barber, "Family Status, Local Community Status and Social Stratification" in *Pacific Sociological Review,* 1961, pp. 3–10, for some useful insights.

7. See Lipset and Bendix, *Social Mobility in Industrial Society,* chap. 2; or P. M. Blau and O. D. Duncan, *The American Occupational Structure* (New York: Wiley, 1967), pp. 86–88.

8. W. J. Reader, *Life in Victorian England* (New York: Capricorn, 1964), pp. 17–37.

9. See G. M. Young, *Victorian England: Portrait of an Age* (London: Harmsworth, 1936), for a superb account of this phenomenon.

10. See Max Weber, *The Protestant Ethic and the Spirit of Capitalism,* trans. Talcott Parsons (various editions exist).

11. See Richard Hofstadter, *The Age of Reform* (New York: Alfred Knopf, 1961).

12. See William Miller and Thomas Cochrane, *Men in Business, Studies in Entrepreneurial History* (New York: Harper Torchbook ed., 1960).

13. Herbert Gutman's unpublished researches on Paterson, N.J., contradict this to some extent, but his materials have not as yet the national sweep of Miller's, or of C. Wright Mills'.

14. Thernstrom, *Poverty and Progress,* pp. 109–111.

15. Bell and Vogel, Introduction to *A Modern Introduction to the Family,* pp. 8–13.

16. Goode, *The Family,* pp. 85, 109, 118.

17. Daniel R. Miller and Guy E. Swanson, *The Changing American Parent* (New York: John Wiley and Sons, 1958); see especially chapter four, and chapter eight, pp. 196–206.

18. Schneider and Homans, "Kinship Terminology and the American Kinship System" in *American Anthropologist,* 47 (1945): 1194–1208.

19. M. Young and P. Wilmott, *Family and Kinship in East London* (London: Routledge and Kegan Paul, 1961); see also Elizabeth Bott, *Family and Social Network* (London: Tavistock Publ., 1957).

20. "Notes" in *The Sociological Quarterly,* 3 (1962): 141–145.

21. Eugene Litwak, "Occupational Mobility and Extended Family Cohesion," *American Sociological Review,* 25 (February 1960); Litwak, "The Use of Extended Family Groups in the Achievement of Social Goals," *Social Problems,* 7 (1959–1960): 177–186. Marvin Sussman, "The Help Pattern in the Middle-Class Family," *American Sociological Review,* 18 (February 1953): 22–28; Sussman, "Family Continuity: Selective Factors Which Affect Relationship between Families at Generation Levels," *Marriage and Family Living,* 16 (May 1954): 112–120.

22. Robert P. Stuckert, "Occupational Mobility and Family Relationships," *Social Forces,* 41.3 (March 1963): 301–307.

23. In *Social Problems,* 6.4 (1959): 333–339.

24. See Scott Greer, *The Emerging City* (Glencoe, Illinois: The Free Press, 1962).

25. Sussman, in *Social Problems,* 6.4 (1959): 336.

INDEX

RICHARD SENNETT was born in Chicago in 1943, and took his bachelor's degree at the University of Chicago (1964) and his Ph.D. at Harvard (1969). Now a Professor of Urban Studies at The Institute for Advanced Study at Princeton University, he is the author of *The Uses of Disorder,* co-author of *The Hidden Injuries of Class* and *Nineteenth Century Cities,* and editor of *Classic Essays on the Culture of Cities.* He lives in New York City.

VINTAGE POLITICAL SCIENCE AND SOCIAL CRITICISM

VINTAGE HISTORY—AMERICAN

VINTAGE HISTORY—WORLD